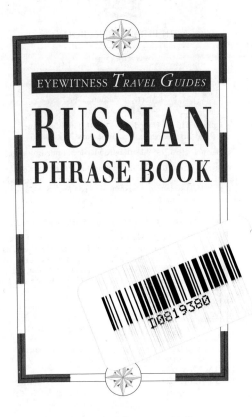

EYEWITNESS *Travel Guides*

RUSSIAN
PHRASE BOOK

A DK Publishing Book

A DK PUBLISHING BOOK

www.dk.com

Compiled by Lexus Ltd with Geoffrey and Ekaterina Smith

First American Edition, 1998

2 4 6 8 10 9 7 5 3

Published in the United States by DK Publishing, Inc.
95 Madison Avenue, New York, New York 10016

DK Publishing books are available at special discounts for bulk purchases
for sales promotions or premiums. Special editions, including personalized
covers, excerpts of existing guides, and corporate imprints can be created
in large quantities for specific needs. For more information, contact
Special Markets Dept./DK Publishing, Inc./95 Madison Ave./New York,
NY 10016/Fax: 800-600-9098.

Library of Congress Cataloging-in-Publication Data
Russian. -- 1st American ed.
    p.   cm. -- (Eyewitness travel guides phrase books)
ISBN 0–7894–3594–2
1. Russian language--Conversation and phrase books--
English.   I. DK Publishing, Inc.   II. Series.
PG2121.R786   1998
491.783'421--DC21   98–16725
                                                            CIP

Printed and bound in Italy by Printer Trento Srl.

CONTENTS

PREFACE

This *Eyewitness Travel Guide Phrase Book* has been compiled
by experts to meet the general needs of tourists and business
travelers. Arranged under headings such as Hotels, Driving,
and so forth, the ample selection of useful words and phrases
is supported by a 2,000-line mini-dictionary. There is also an
extensive menu guide listing approximately 300 dishes or
methods of cooking and presentation.

Typical replies to questions you may ask during your trip,
and the signs or instructions you may see or hear, are shown
in tinted boxes. In the main text, the pronunciation of Russian
words and phrases is imitated in English sound syllables.
There is a comprehensive guide to Russian pronunciation at
the beginning of the book.

Eyewitness Travel Guides are recognized as the world's best
travel guides. Each title features specially commissioned color
photographs, cutaways of major buildings, 3-D aerial views,
and detailed maps, plus information on sights, events, hotels,
restaurants, shopping, and entertainment.

Eyewitness Travel Guides titles include:
Moscow · St. Petersburg · Amsterdam · Australia · Sydney
Budapest · California · Florida · Hawaii · New York
San Francisco & Northern California · France · Loire Valley · Paris
Provence · Great Britain · London · Ireland · Dublin · Scotland
Greece: Athens & the Mainland · The Greek Islands · Istanbul
Italy · Florence & Tuscany · Naples · Rome · Sardinia
Venice & the Veneto · Mexico · Portugal · Lisbon · Prague
South Africa · Spain · Barcelona · Madrid · Seville & Andalusia
Thailand · Vienna · Warsaw

PRONUNCIATION

When reading the imitated pronunciation, stress the part that is underlined. Pronounce each syllable as if it formed part of an English word and you will be understood fairly well. Remember the points below, and your pronunciation will be even closer to the correct Russian:

a	as in "alimony"
ay	as in "may"
e	as in "egg"
I	as in "die"
i	as in "lid"
kh	a guttural "ch" as in the Scottish pronunciation of "loch"
o	as in "rob"
oy	as in "boy"
ye	as in "yet"
zh	as "s" in "leisure" but harder
'	no sound of its own but softens the preceding consonant and adds a slight y sound, e.g., *n'* would sound like *ny* as in "canyon."

The mini-dictionary (pages 104–126) provides the Russian translations in the form of the imitated pronunciation so you can read the words without reference to the Russian alphabet. In the phrases, the abbreviations *(m)* and *(f)* indicate the forms to be used by a male or female speaker, respectively.

On the next page is a further guide to Russian pronunciation, along with the Russian (Cyrillic) alphabet.

THE RUSSIAN (CYRILLIC) ALPHABET

letter		pronunciation
А	а	(a) as in "alimony"
Б	б	(b) as in "bed"
В	в	(v) as in "vet"
Г	г	(g) as in "get"
Д	д	(d) as in "debt"
Е	е	(ye) as in "yet"
Ё	ё	(yo) as in "yonder"
Ж	ж	(zh) as "s" in "leisure" but harder
З	з	(z) as in "zither"
И	и	(ee) as in "see"
Й	й	(y) as in "boy"
К	к	(k) as in "king"
Л	л	(l) as in "loot"
М	м	(m) as in "match"
Н	н	(n) as in "never"
О	о	(o) as in "rob"
П	п	(p) as in "pea"
Р	р	(r) as in "rat-a-tat"
С	с	(s) as in "lass"

letter		pronunciation
Т	т	(t) as in "toffee"
У	у	(oo) as in "boot"
Ф	ф	(f) as in "fellow"
Х	х	(kh) as a guttural "ch"
Ц	ц	(ts) as in "let's"
Ч	ч	(ch) as in "chair"
Ш	ш	(sh) as in "shovel"
Щ	щ	(shsh) as above but with a slight roll, as in "fresh sheet"
Ъ	ъ	hard sign – no sound but use very slight pause before next letter
Ы	ы	(i) approximately as in "lid"
Ь	ь	soft sign – no sound but softens preceding consonant
Э	э	(e) as in "egg"
Ю	ю	(you) as in "youth"
Я	я	(ya) as in "yak"

USEFUL EVERYDAY PHRASES

Yes/No
Да/нет
da/nyet

Thank you
Спасибо
spaseeba

No, thank you
Нет, спасибо
nyet, spaseeba

Please
Пожалуйста
pazhalsta

I don't understand
Я не понимаю
ya nye paneema-yoo

Do you speak English?
Вы говорите по-английски?
vi gavareet-ye pa-angleeskee?

I can't speak Russian
Я не говорю по-русски
ya nye gavaryoo pa-rooskee

I don't know
Я не знаю
ya nye zna-yoo

Please speak more slowly
Пожалуйста, говорите медленнее
pazhalsta, gavareet-ye myedlyenye-ye

Please write it down for me
Пожалуйста, напишите это мне
pazhalsta, napeesheet-ye eta mnye

My name is …
Меня зовут …
myenya zavoot …

How do you do, pleased to meet you
Здравствуйте, очень приятно
zdrastvooyt-ye, ochen' pree-yatna

Good morning
Доброе утро
dobra-ye ootra

Good afternoon
Добрый день
dobri dyen'

Good evening
Добрый вечер
dobri vyechyer

Good night *(when going to bed)*
Спокойной ночи
spakoynay nochee

Good night *(leaving group early)*
Счастливо оставаться
shasleeva astavatsa

Good-bye
До свидания
da sveedanya

How are you?
Как дела?
kak dyela?

Excuse me, please
Извините, пожалуйста
eezveeneet-ye, pazhalsta

Sorry!
Простите!
prasteet-ye!

I'm really sorry
Я очень сожалею
ya ochen' sozhalyeyou

Can you help me?
Вы можете мне помочь?
vi mozhet-ye mnye pamoch'?

Can you tell me …?
Скажите, пожалуйста …
skazheet-ye, pazhalsta …

Can I have …?
Можно …?
mozhna …?

I would like …
Я хотел (*m*)/хотела (*f*) бы …
ya khatyel/khatyela bi …

Is there … here?
Здесь есть ...?
zdyes' yest' …?

Where can I get …?
Где можно найти ...?
Gdye mozhna nItee …?

How much is it?
Сколько это стоит?
skol'ka eta sto-eet?

What time is it?
Который час?
katori chas?

I must go now
Мне пора идти
mnye para eetee

I'm lost
Я заблудился (*m*)/заблудилась (*f*)
ya zabloodeelsa/zabloodeelas'

Cheers! (*toast*)
Ваше здоровье!
vashe zdarov'ye!

Do you take credit cards?
Вы принимаете кредитные карточки?
vi preeneema-yet-ye kryedeetniye kartachkee?

Where is the restroom?
Где туалет?
gdye too-alyet?

Go away!
Уходите!
ookhad<u>ee</u>t-ye!

Excellent!
Отлично!
atl<u>ee</u>chna!

THINGS YOU'LL HEAR

astar<u>o</u>zhna!	Look out!
ay!	Hey!
da sveed<u>a</u>nya	Good-bye
eezveen<u>ee</u>t-ye	Excuse me
kak dy<u>e</u>la?	How are you?
kharash<u>o</u>, spas<u>ee</u>ba, a vi?	Fine, thank you—and you?
oov<u>ee</u>deemsa	See you later
pazh<u>a</u>lsta	You're welcome
pr<u>a</u>vda?	Is that so?
pr<u>a</u>veel'na	That's right
shto, prast<u>ee</u>t-ye?	Excuse me?
spas<u>ee</u>ba	Thanks
vot, pazh<u>a</u>lsta	Here you are
ya nye paneem<u>a</u>-yoo	I don't understand
ya nye zn<u>a</u>-yoo	I don't know
zdr<u>a</u>stvooyt-ye, <u>o</u>chen' pr<u>e</u>yatna	How do you do, nice to meet you

THINGS YOU'LL SEE

вода для питья	*vada dlya peet'ya*	drinking water
вход	*fkhot*	entrance
вход воспрещён	*fkhot vaspryeshyon*	no entrance
входите	*fkhadeet-ye*	come directly in
вход свободный	*fkhot svabodni*	free admission
выход	*vikhat*	exit
Ж/женский туалет	*zhenskee too-alyet*	women's restroom
заказано	*zakazana*	reserved
закрыто	*zakrita*	closed
занято	*zanyata*	occupied
запасной выход	*zapasnoy vikhot*	emergency exit
Интурист	*eentooreest*	Intourist
касса	*kasa*	cash register
к себе	*ksyeb-ye*	pull
лифт	*leeft*	elevator
М		subway; men's restroom
мужской туалет	*mooshskoy tooalyet*	men's restroom
осторожно, окрашено	*astarozhna, akrashyena*	caution, wet paint
открыто	*atkrita*	open
от себя	*atsyebya*	push
пожарный выход	*pazharni vikhat*	fire exit
посторонним вход воспрещён	*pastaroneem fkhot vaspryeshyon*	private/no entrance
рынок	*rinak*	market
соблюдайте тишину	*sablyoodalt-ye teesheenoo*	silence/quiet
туалеты	*too-alyeti*	restroom
часы работы	*chasi raboti*	opening times

DAYS, MONTHS, SEASONS

Sunday	воскресенье	*vaskryesyen'ye*
Monday	понедельник	*panyedyel'neek*
Tuesday	вторник	*ftorneek*
Wednesday	среда	*sryeda*
Thursday	четверг	*chyetvyerk*
Friday	пятница	*pyatneetsa*
Saturday	суббота	*soobota*
January	январь	*yanvar'*
February	февраль	*fyevral'*
March	март	*mart*
April	апрель	*apryel'*
May	май	*ml*
June	июнь	*ee-yoon'*
July	июль	*ee-yool'*
August	август	*avgoost*
September	сентябрь	*syentyabr'*
October	октябрь	*aktyabr'*
November	ноябрь	*na-yabr'*
December	декабрь	*dyekabr'*
Spring	весна	*vyesna*
Summer	лето	*lyeta*
Autumn	осень	*osyen'*
Winter	зима	*zeema*
Christmas	Рождество	*razhdyestvo*
Christmas Eve	Сочельник	*sachyel'neek*
New Year	Новый год	*novi god*
New Year's Eve	Новогодняя ночь	*navagodnya-ya noch'*

NUMBERS

0 ноль *nol'*

1 один/одна/одно
adeen/adna/adno

2 два/две *dva/dvye*

3 три *tree*

4 четыре *chyetir-ye*

5 пять *pyat'*

6 шесть *shest'*

7 семь *syem'*

8 восемь *vosyem'*

9 девять *dyevyat'*

10 десять *dyesyat'*

11 одиннадцать *adeenatsat'*

12 двенадцать *dvyenatsat'*

13 тринадцать *treenatsat'*

14 четырнадцать *chyetirnatsat'*

15 пятнадцать *pyatnatsat'*

16 шестнадцать *shesnatsat'*

17 семнадцать *syemnatsat'*

18 восемнадцать *vasyemnatsat'*

19 девятнадцать *dyevyatnatsat'*

20 двадцать *dvatsat'*

21 двадцать один *dvatsat' adeen*

22 двадцать два *dvatsat' dva*

30 тридцать *treetsat'*

31 тридцать один *treetsat' adeen*

32 тридцать два *treetsat' dva*

40 сорок *sorak*

50 пятьдесят *pyadyesyat*

60 шестьдесят *shesdyesyat*

70 семьдесят *syem'dyesyat*

80 восемьдесят *vosyem'dyesyat*

90 девяносто *dyevyanosta*

100 сто *sto adeen*

110 сто десять *sto dyesyat'*

200 двести *dvyestee*

300 триста *treesta*

400 четыреста *chyetiryesta*
500 пятьсот *pyat'sot*
600 шестьсот *shes'ot*
700 семьсот *syem'sot*
800 восемьсот *vasyem'sot*
900 девятьсот *dyevyat'sot*
1,000 тысяча *tisyacha*
10,000 десять тысяч *dyesyat' tisyach*
20,000 двадцать тысяч *dvatsat' tisyach*
100,000 сто тысяч *sto tisyach*
1,000,000 миллион *meelee-on*

Ordinal Numbers

1st первое *pyerva-ye*
2nd второе *ftaro-ye*
3rd третье *tryet'ye*
4th четвёртое *chyetvyorta-ye*
5th пятое *pyata-ye*
6th шестое *shesto-ye*
7th седьмое *cyed'mo-ye*
8th восьмое *vas'mo-ye*
9th девятое *dyevyata-ye*
10th десятое *dyesyata-ye*
11th одиннадцатое *adeenatsata-ye*
12th двенадцатое *dvyenatsata-ye*
13th тринадцатое *treenatsata-ye*
14th четырнадцатое *chyetirnatsata-ye*
15th пятнадцатое *pyatnatsata-ye*
16th шестнадцатое *shesnatsata-ye*
17th семнадцатое *cyemnatsata-ye*
18th восемнадцатое *vasyemnatsata-ye*
19th девятнадцатое *dyevyatnatsata-ye*
20th двадцатое *dvatsata-ye*
21st двадцать первое *dvatsat' pyerva-ye*
30th тридцатое *treetsata-ye*
31st тридцать первое *treetsat' pyerva-ye*

TIME

today	сегодня	*syevodnya*
yesterday	вчера	*fchyera*
tomorrow	завтра	*zaftra*
the day before yesterday	позавчера	*pazafchyera*
the day after tomorrow	послезавтра	*paslyezaftra*
this week	на этой неделе	*na etay nyedyel-ye*
last week	на прошлой неделе	*na proshlay nyedyel-ye*
next week	на следующей неделе	*na slyedoo-yooshay nyedyel-ye*
this morning	сегодня утром	*syevodnya ootram*
this afternoon	сегодня днём	*syevodnya dnyom*
this evening/ tonight	сегодня вечером	*syevodnya vyechyeram*
yesterday afternoon	вчера днём	*fchyera dnyom*
last night (*before midnight*)	вчера вечером	*fchyera vyechyerom*
last night (*after midnight*)	вчера ночью	*fchyera noch'yoo*
tomorrow morning	завтра утром	*zaftra ootram*
tomorrow night	завтра вечером	*zaftra vyechyerom*
in three days	через три дня	*chyeryez tree dnya*
three days ago	три дня назад	*tree dnya nazat*
late	поздно	*pozna*
early	рано	*rana*
soon	скоро	*skora*
later on	позже	*pozhe*
at the moment	сейчас	*syaychas*
second	секунда	*syekoonda*
minute	минута	*meenoota*
one minute	одна минута	*adna meenoota*
two minutes	две минуты	*dvye meenooti*

quarter of an hour	четверть часа	*chyetvyert' chasa*
half an hour	полчаса	*polchasa*
three quarters of an hour	три четверти часа	*tree chyetvyertee chasa*
hour	час	*chas*
that day	этот день	*etat dyen,*
every day	каждый день	*kazhdi dyen'*
all day	весь день	*vyes' dyen'*
the next day	следующий день	*slyedoo-yooshee dyen'*

TELLING TIME

One o'clock is час (*chas*); for two, three, and four o'clock use the number followed by часа (*chasa*); the remaining hours to twelve o'clock are simply the appropriate number plus the word часов (*chasov*).

For time past the hour, e.g., one twenty, Russians say двадцать минут второго (*dvatsat' meenoot ftarova*), meaning literally "twenty minutes of the second (hour)."

Quarter after one and one thirty are also expressed as being "of the following (hour)." Quarter after one is therefore четверть второго (*chyetvyert' ftarova*) and two thirty is половина третьего (*palaveena tryet'yeva*).

For time "of" the hour, Russians use без (*byez*), meaning "less," e.g., ten of three is без десяти три (*byez dyesyatee tree*), literally "less ten three."

The 24-hour clock is commonly used, in particular for timetables. Cross-reference to the number section on page 15 may be helpful.

AM	утра	*ootra*
PM	дня	*dnya*
one o'clock	час	*chas*
ten after one	десять минут второго	*dyesyat' meenoot ftarova*

quarter after one	четверть второго	*chyetvyert' ftarova*
one thirty	половина второго	*palaveena ftarova*
twenty of two	без двадцати два	*byez dvatsatee dva*
quarter of two	без четверти два	*byez chyetvyertee dva*
two o'clock	два часа	*dva chasa*
13:00	тринадцать ноль-ноль	*treenatsat' nol'-nol'*
16:30	шестнадцать тридцать	*shesnatsat' treetsat'*
at five thirty	в половине шестого	*fpalaveen-ye shestova*
at seven o'clock	в семь часов	*fsyem' cha'sof*
noon	полдень	*poldyen'*
midnight	полночь	*polnach'*

HOTELS

In recent years the choice and quality of hotel accommodations in large Russian cities have improved significantly with the emergence of Western-managed hotels. While these offer, in general, excellent service, they are quite expensive, and a typical package tour is more likely to involve a traditional Intourist hotel, especially outside the big cities. This kind of package tour will usually include a generous, if not culinarily varied, breakfast, lunch, and dinner, plus a room with a private bathroom and telephone. Standards of service, courtesy, and cleanliness vary, but, compared to those of American hotels, are not likely to be more than adequate. On each floor of the hotel, there will be a дежурная (*dyezhoorna-ya*), or floor-lady, acting as a receptionist. The floor-lady has custody of the keys and will issue a key pass which you will need to show when collecting the key. She will also be able to help with any problem concerning your accommodations or laundry, or simply to make you a cup of tea.

Although it is now possible for foreigners to travel outside their principal area of residence (within the Russian Federation) without additional endorsement of their visa, advice should still be sought from your tour representative, since some towns remain "closed" to foreign visitors.

Even if you are paying for your hotel accommodations with a credit card, you should always have a certain amount of foreign currency with you (preferably US dollars). You will need to exchange quite a lot of this foreign currency during your stay in Russia because stores, restaurants, and bars will now only accept payment in roubles. Taxi drivers, however, may still expect you to pay in dollars.

Throughout the day it is possible to have a light snack and tea or coffee in one of the hotel cafeterias. Travelers requiring a vegetarian menu should notify the tour guide or inform the hotel staff when checking in.

USEFUL WORDS AND PHRASES

balcony	балкон	*balkon*
bathroom	ванная	*vana-ya*
bed	кровать	*kravat'*
bedroom	спальня	*spal'nya*
bill	счёт	*shyot*
breakfast	завтрак	*zaftrak*
dining room	столовая	*stalova-ya*
dinner	ужин	*oozheen*
double room	номер с	*nomyer sdvoo-*
	двуспальной	*spal'nay*
	кроватью	*kravat'-yoo*
elevator	лифт	*leeft*
floor-lady	дежурная	*dyezhoorna-ya*
foyer	фойе	*fay-ye*
full board	проживание с	*prazheevaneeye*
	трёхразовым	*stryokh-razovim*
	питанием	*peetaneeyem*
half board	проживание с	*prazheevaneeye*
	двухразовым	*sdvookh-razovim*
	питанием	*peetaneeyem*
hotel	гостиница	*gasteeneetsa*
key	ключ	*klyooch*
lunch	обед	*abyet*
manager	администратор	*admeeneestratar*
reception	регистратура	*ryegeestratoora*
restaurant	ресторан	*ryestaran*
room	номер	*nomyer*
room service	комнатное	*komnatna-ye*
	обслуживание	*absloozheevaneeye*
shower	душ	*doosh*
single room	одноместный	*adnamyestni*
	номер	*nomyer*
toilet	туалет	*too-alyet*
twin room	двухместный	*dvookhmyestni*
	номер	*nomyer*

21

Do you have a larger/brighter room?
У вас есть номер побольше/посветлее?
oo vas yest' nomyer pabol'shye/pasvyetlyeye?

May I please have the key for room number …?
Дайте, пожалуйста, ключ от номера …
dayt-ye, pazhalsta, klooch ot nomyera …

There has been some mistake; I asked for a double room
Произошла ошибка, я просил (*m*)/просила (*f*) номер с
    двуспальной кроватью
*pra-eezashla asheepka, ya praseel/praseela nomyer sdvoo-spal'nay
    kravat'yoo*

I'd prefer a room with a balcony
Я предпочёл (*m*)/предпочла (*f*) бы номер с балконом
ya pryedpachyol/pryedpachla bi nomyer sbalkonam

The window in my room is jammed
Окно в моём номере не открывается
akno vmayom nomyer-ye nye atkriva-yetsa

The shower doesn't work
Душ не работает
doosh nye rabota-yet

The bathroom light doesn't work
В ванной нет света
v-vanay nyet svyeta

May I have another light bulb?
Дайте другую лампочку
dayt-ye droogooyoo lampachkoo

There is no hot water/toilet paper
Нет горячей воды/туалетной бумаги
nyet garyachyay vadi/ too-alyetnay boomagee

What is the charge per night?
Сколько стоит номер за ночь?
skol'ka sto-eet nomyer zanach'?

When is breakfast?
Когда завтрак?
kagda zaftrak?

Would you have my baggage brought up?
Будьте добры, принесите мой багаж
bood't-ye dabri, preenyeseet-ye moy bagazh

Please call me at … o'clock
Пожалуйста, позвоните мне в … часов
pazhalsta, pazvaneet-ye mnye v … chasof

Can I have breakfast in my room?
Можно завтракать в номере?
mozhna zavtrakat' vnomyer-ye?

I'll be back at … o'clock
Я вернусь в …
ya vyernoos' v …

My room number is …
Мой номер …
moy nomyer …

I'm leaving tomorrow
Я уезжаю завтра
ya oo-yezha-yoo zavtra

When do I have to vacate my room?
Когда надо освободить номер?
kagda nada asvabadeet' nomyer?

May I have the bill, please?
Счёт, пожалуйста
shyot, pazhalsta

I'll pay by credit card
Я заплачу кредитной карточкой
ya zaplachoo kryedeetnay kartachkay

I'll pay cash
Я заплачу наличными
ya zaplachoo naleechnimee

Can you get me a taxi?
Вы можете вызвать мне такси?
vi mozhet-ye vizvat' mn-ye taksee?

Thank you for all your help
Спасибо за вашу помощь
spaseeba za vashoo pomash'

THINGS YOU'LL HEAR

eezveeneet-ye, myest nyet
I'm sorry, we have no vacancies

adna-myestnikh namyerof bol'shye nyet
There are no single rooms left

dvookh-myestnikh namyerof bol'shye nyet
There are no double rooms left

na skol'ka nachay?
For how many nights?

THINGS YOU'LL SEE

бар	*bar*	bar
ванная	*vana-ya*	bath
гостиница	*gasteeneetsa*	hotel
номер с двуспальной кроватью	*nomyer sdvoo-spal'nay kravat'-yoo*	double room
душ	*doosh*	shower
завтрак	*zaftrak*	breakfast
заказ	*zakas*	reservation
запасной выход	*zapasnoy vikhat*	emergency exit
к себе	*ksyeb-ye*	pull
лифт	*leeft*	elevator
двухместный номер	*dvookh-myestni nomyer*	twin room
обед	*abyet*	lunch
одноместный номер	*adna-myestni nomyer*	single room
от себя	*atsyebya*	push
первый этаж	*pyervi etash*	ground floor
пожарный выход	*pazharni vikat*	fire exit
проживание с двухразовым питанием	*prazheevaneeye sdvookh-razavim peetanee-yem*	half board
проживание с трехразовым питанием	*prazheevaneeye stryokh-razavim peetaneeyem*	full board
регистратура	*ryegeestratoora*	reception
ресторан	*ryestaran*	restaurant
счёт	*shyot*	bill
туалет/W.C.	*too-alyet*	restroom
1		ground floor (as shown on elevator button)

DRIVING

Apart from the usual documentation, i.e., an international driver's license (with enclosure in Russian) and insurance documentation, you will also need a car registration document and Intourist vehicle documentation. The latter will contain details of your itinerary and all stopovers (as previously arranged). It will include vouchers for prepaid accommodations and a car sticker showing your country of origin.

Rough road conditions and relatively few auto-body shops make it essential that you carry sufficient spare parts in case you have to do your own repairs. Some important items to take are a tow rope, engine oil, brake fluid, jump start cables, spark plugs, spare windshield wipers, spare bulbs, points, fuses, antifreeze in winter, and a luminous warning triangle to place on the road if you do break down. Because it cannot be taken for granted that all gas stations sell the right gas for your car, it is also worth taking a couple of cans of gas, stocking up when you can and thus always having emergency supplies with you.

On the open road, international (diagrammatic) road signs are used. The traffic police are called ГАИ (*Ga-ee*), which stands for State Automobile Inspectorate. If you are lost or in need of assistance, they can sometimes be helpful. Drive on the right and pass on the left. On main roads outside of towns the speed limit is generally 90 km/h (55 mph), and in town it is generally 60 km/h (35 mph). Front-seat passengers must wear their seat belts. It is a crime to drive a car after drinking any alcohol.

SOME COMMON ROAD SIGNS

автостанция	*avta-stantsee-ya*	auto-body shop
автостоянка	*avta-stayanka*	parking lot
автострада	*avta-strada*	highway

→

бензоколонка	*byenzakalonka*	gas station
берегись поезда	*byeryegees' poyezda*	beware of trains
включить фары	*vklyoocheet' fari*	headlights on
внимание!	*vneemaneeye!*	watch out!
вход воспрещён	*vkhod vaspryeshyon*	no trespassing
выключить фары	*vyklyoocheet' fari*	headlights off
въезд запрещен	*v-yezd zapryeshyon*	no entry
гололёд	*galalyot*	sheet ice
держитесь левой стороны	*dyerzheetyes' lyevay starani*	(pedestrians) keep to the left
дорожные работы	*darozhniye raboti*	road work
ж/д переезд	*zhe de pyerye-yezd*	train crossing
железно- дорожный переезд	*zhelyezna- darozhni pyerye-yezd*	train crossing
зона	*zona*	zone
конец автострады	*kanyets avta-stradi*	end of highway
медленно	*myedlyenna*	slow
не обгонять	*nye abganyat'*	no passing
объезд	*ab-yezd*	detour
одностороннее движение	*adna-staronyeye dveezhyeneeye*	one-way street
опасно	*apasna*	danger
опасный перекрёсток	*apasni pyeryekryostak*	dangerous intersection
опасный поворот	*apasni pavarot*	dangerous bend
осторожно	*astarozhna*	caution
перекрёсток	*pyeryekryostak*	intersection
пешеходы	*pyeshekhodi*	pedestrians
подземный переход	*padzyemni pyeryekhot*	underground passage
скользко	*skol'zka*	slippery surface
скорая помощь	*skora-ya pomash'*	first aid
станция тех- обслуживания	*stantsee-ya tyekh- absloozheevanee-ya*	service station

→

27

стоянка запрещена	*stayanka zapryeshyena*	no parking
центр города	*tsyentr gorada*	town center
школа	*shkola*	school

USEFUL WORDS AND PHRASES

antifreeze	антифриз	*unteefreez*
auto body shop	автостанция	*avta-stantsee-ya*
automatic	автоматический	*avta-mateechyeskee*
brake (*noun*)	тормоз	*tormas*
breakdown	поломка	*palomka*
camper (*trailer*)	дом-автофургон	*dom-avtafoorgon*
car	машина	*masheena*
clutch	сцепление	*stsyeplyeneeye*
drive (*verb*)	водить машину	*vadeet' masheenoo*
driver's manual	автомобильный справочник	*avtamabeel'ni spravachneek*
engine	мотор	*mator*
exhaust	выхлопная труба	*vikhlapna-ya trooba*
fanbelt	вентиляционный ремень	*vyenteelyatsee-oni ryemyen'*
gas	бензин	*byenzeen*
gas station	бензоколонка	*byenzakalonka*
gear	передача	*pyeryedacha*
headlights	фары	*fari*
highway	автострада	*avta-strada*
intersection	перекрёсток	*pyeryekryostak*
junction (*on highway*)	развилка	*razveelka*
license	водительские права	*vadeetyel'skeeye prava*
license plate	номерной знак	*namyernoy znak*
mirror	зеркало	*zyerkala*
motorcycle	мотоцикл	*matatseekl*

road	дорога	*daroga*
skid (*verb*)	заносить	*zanaseet'*
spare parts	запчасти	*zapchastee*
speed (*noun*)	скорость	*skorast'*
speed limit	ограничение скорости	*agraneechyeneeye skorastee*
speedometer	спидометр	*speedomyetr*
steering wheel	руль	*rool'*
taillights	задние фонари	*zadneeye fanaree*
tire	шина	*sheena*
tow	буксировать	*bookseeravat'*
traffic lights	светофор	*svyetafor*
trailer	прицеп	*preetsyep*
truck	грузовик	*groozaveek*
trunk	багажник	*bagazhneek*
van	фургон	*foorgon*
wheel	колесо	*kalyeso*
windshield	переднее стекло	*pyeryednyeye styeklo*

I'd like some oil/water
Мне нужно масло/нужна вода
mnye noozhna masla/noozhna vada

Fill her up, please!
Полный бак, пожалуйста!
polni bak, pazhalsta!

I'd like 10 liters of gas
Мне нужно 10 литров бензина
mnye noozhna dyesyat' leetraf byenzeena

Would you check the tires, please?
Проверьте шины, пожалуйста
pravyer't-ye sheeni, pazhalsta

Do you do repairs?
Здесь можно починить машину?
zdyes' mozhna pacheeneet' masheenoo?

Can you repair the brakes?
Вы можете починить тормоза?
vi mozhet-ye pacheeneet' tarmaza?

How long will it take?
Сколько времени это займёт?
skol'ka vryemyenee eta zImyot?

Where can I park?
Где можно поставить машину?
gdye mozhna pastaveet' masheenoo?

Can I park here?
Можно здесь поставить машину?
mozhna zdyes' pastaveet' masheenoo?

There's something wrong with the engine
Что-то случилось с мотором
shto-ta sloocheelas' smatoram

The engine is overheating
Мотор перегревается
mator pyerye-gryeva-yetsa

I need a new tire
Мне нужна новая шина
mnye noozhna nova-ya sheena

I'd like to rent a car
Я хочу взять напрокат машину
ya khachoo vzyat' naprakat masheenoo

Where is the nearest auto-body shop?
Где ближайшая автостанция?
gdye bleezhIsha-ya avta-stantsee-ya?

How do I get to …?
Как доехать до ...?
kak da-yekhat' do …?

Is this the road to …?
Это дорога в ...?
eta daroga v …?

DIRECTIONS YOU MAY BE GIVEN

pryama	straight ahead
slyeva	on the left
pavyerneet-ye nalyeva	turn left
sprava	on the right
pavyerneet-ye naprava	turn right
pyervi pavarot naprava	first on the right
ftaroy pavarot nalyeva	second on the left
posl-ye …	past the …

THINGS YOU'LL HEAR

vi khateet-ye avta-mateechyeskee eelee roochnoy?
Would you like an automatic or a manual?

pakazheet-ye vash prava
May I see your license?

THINGS YOU'LL SEE

бензин	*byenzeen*	gas
выход	*vikhot*	exit
давление в шинах	*davlyeneeye vsheenakh*	tire pressure
дизель	*deezyel'*	diesel
масло	*masla*	oil
развилка	*razveelka*	highway junction
ремонт	*ryemont*	repair

TRAIN TRAVEL

Train travel in Russia will give even the most sanitized tour package a true flavor of the grime of day-to-day conditions and the magnificent warmth of the people who live in them. Apart from transporting you from point A to point B, train trips should also be seized as an excellent opportunity for getting to know Russians and speaking Russian with them.

On long distance journeys, tourists will travel in мягкий (*myakhkee*, literally "soft") compartments with two sleeping berths, or in купе (*koope*, literally "coupé") compartments with four sleeping berths. All compartments are nonsmoking unless passengers agree to the contrary.

The carriage attendant is there as a sort of maître d'hôtel cum chambermaid. He or she is responsible for (and house-proud of) the cleanliness of the carriage, and also makes up the beds, sorts out rowdy passengers, and serves tea. When not busy working (and frequently when they are), they often enjoy a good chat.

To avoid wasting time buying tickets for long-distance trips, it is always worth reserving a seat through Intourist. Buying tickets for suburban trains, on the other hand, can be done as easily as in the West.

USEFUL WORDS AND PHRASES

baggage cart	тележка для багажа	*tyelyezhka dlya bagazha*
baggage rack	багажная полка	*bagazhna-ya polka*
baggage room	камера хранения	*kamyera khranyenee-ya*
baggage van	багажное отделение	*bagazhna-ye atdyelyeneeye*
buffet	буфет	*boofyet*
carriage	вагон	*vagon*
compartment	купе	*koope*
connection	пересадка	*pyeryesadka*

dining car	вагон-ресторан	*vagon-ryestaran*
emergency cord	стоп-кран	*stop-kran*
entrance	вход	*fkhot*
exit	выход	*vikhot*
get in	входить	*fkhadeet'*
get out	выходить	*vikhadeet'*
guard	проводник	*pravadneek*
lost and found office	бюро находок	*byooro nakhodak*
one-way ticket	билет в один конец	*beelyet vadeen kanyets*
platform	платформа	*platforma*
railroad	железная дорога	*zhelyezna-ya daroga*
reservation office	касса	*kasa*
reserved seat	забронированное место	*zabraneeravano-ye myesta*
restaurant car	вагон-ресторан	*vagon-ryestaran*
round-trip ticket	обратный билет	*abratni beelyet*
schedule board	табло	*tablo*
seat	место	*myesta*
sleeping car	спальный вагон	*spal'ni vagon*
station *(main-line terminal)*	вокзал	*vagzal*
station *(all other stations including subway)*	станция	*stantsee-ya*
station master	начальник вокзала	*nachal'neek vagzala*
ticket	билет	*beelyet*
ticket collector	контролёр	*kantralyor*
timetable	расписание	*raspeesaneeye*
tracks	пути	*pootee*
train *(by train)*	поезд поездом	*po-yest po-yezdam*
waiting room	зал ожидания	*zal azheedanee-ya*
window	окно	*akno*

When does the train for ... leave?
Когда отходит поезд в ...?
kagda atkhodeet po-yest v ...?

When does the train from ... arrive?
Когда приходит поезд из ...?
kagda preekhodeet po-yest eez ...?

When is the next train to ...?
Когда следующий поезд в ...?
kagda slyedoo-yoo-shee po-yest v ...?

When is the first train to ...?
Когда первый поезд в ...?
kagda pyervi po-yest v ...?

When is the last train to ...?
Когда последний поезд в ...?
kagda paslyednee po-yest v ...?

What is the fare to ...?
Сколько стоит проезд до ...?
skol'ka sto-eet pro-yest do ...?

Do I have to change?
Мне нужно делать пересадку?
mnye noozhna dyelat' pyeryesadkoo?

Does the train stop at ...?
Поезд останавливается в ...?
po-yest astanavleeva-yetsa v ...?

How long does it take to get to ...?
Сколько времени нужно ехать до ...?
skolka vryemyenee noozhna yekhat' do ...?

A round-trip ticket to …, please
Обратный билет до ..., пожалуйста
abratni beelyet do …, pazhalsta

Do I have to pay a supplement?
Я должен (m)/должна (f) доплатить?
ya dolzhen/dalzhna daplateet'?

I'd like to reserve a seat
Я хочу заказать место
ya khachoo zakazat' myesta

Is this the right train for …?
Это поезд до ...?
eta po-yest do …?

Is this the right platform for the … train?
С этой платформы отходит поезд до ...?
setay platformi atkhodeet po-yest do …?

Which platform for the … train?
С какой платформы отходит поезд до ...?
skakoy platfor,mi atkhodeet po-yest do …?

Is the train late?
Поезд опаздывает?
po-yest apazdiva-yet?

Could you help me with my baggage, please?
Вы не поможете мне с багажом, пожалуйста
vi nye pamozhet-ye mnye sbagazhom, pazhalsta

Is this seat free?
Это место свободно?
eta myesta svabodna?

This seat is taken
Это место занято
eta myesta zanyata

I have reserved this seat
Я забронировал *(m)*/забронировала *(f)* это место
ya zabraneeravol/zabra neeravala eta myesta

May I open the window?
Можно открыть окно?
mozhna atkrit' akno?

May I close the window?
Можно закрыть окно?
mozhna zakrit' akno?

When do we arrive in …?
Когда мы приезжаем в …?
kagda mi pree-yezha-yem v …?

What station is this?
Какая это станция?
kaka-ya eta stantsee-ya?

What station is this? *(main-line terminal)*
Какой это вокзал?
kakoy eta vagzal?

Do we stop at …?
Мы останавливаемся в …?
mi astanavleeva-yemsa v …?

Would you keep an eye on my things for a moment?
Вы не посмотрите минуту за моими вещами?
vi nye pasmotreet-ye meenootoo za ma-eemee vyeshamee?

Is there a restaurant car on this train?
В этом поезде есть вагон-ресторан?
vetam po-yezd-ye yest' vagon-ryestaran?

THINGS YOU'LL SEE

билетная касса	*beelyetna-ya kasa*	ticket office
билеты	*beelyeti*	tickets
буфет	*boofyet*	snack bar
вагон	*vagon*	carriage
вокзал	*vagzal*	central station (main-line railroad terminal)
воскресенья и выходные дни	*vaskryesyen'ya ee vikhadneeye dnee*	Sundays and public holidays
вход	*fkhot*	entrance
выход	*vikhot*	exit
газеты	*gazyeti*	newspapers
доплата	*daplata*	supplement
задержка	*zadyershka*	delay
зал ожидания	*zal azheedanee-ya*	waiting room
занято	*zanya-ta*	occupied
информация	*eenformatsee-ya*	information
камера хранения	*kamyera khranyenee-ya*	baggage room
к поездам	*k po-yezdam*	to the trains
кроме воскресений	*krom-ye vaskryesyenee*	except Sundays
место для курения	*myesta dlya kooryenee-ya*	smoking permitted
не высовываться из окон	*nye visovivatsa eez okan*	do not lean out of the window
не курить	*nye kooreet'*	no smoking
не останав- ливается в ...	*nye astanav- leeva-yetsa v ...*	does not stop in ...

→

нет входа	*nyet fkhoda*	no entrance
обмен валюты	*abmyen valyooti*	currency exchange
отправление	*atpravlyeneeye*	departures
платформа	*platforma*	platform
поездка	*pa-yestka*	trip, journey
предварительный заказ билетов	*pryedvareetyel'ni zakas beelyetaf*	seat reservation
прибытие	*preebiteeye*	arrivals
пригородный поезд	*preegaradni po-yest*	local train
расписание	*raspeesaneeye*	timetable
свободно	*svabodna*	vacant
спальный вагон	*spal'ni vagon*	sleeping car
стоп-кран	*stop-kran*	emergency cord
только по будним дням	*tol'ka paboodneem dnyam*	weekdays only

THINGS YOU'LL HEAR

vneemaneeye
Attention

beelyeti, pazhalsta
Tickets, please

AIR TRAVEL

More than 300 national and local airlines make internal flights
in Russia. The two biggest among them are Aeroflot and
Transaero. Reservations are usually made through Intourist.
Check that you have all necessary flight information, and if in
doubt ask Intourist to provide you with flight details in
English and, if possible, in writing.

Before making arrangements to fly in Russia, you should
check that your visa permits you to travel wherever you want
to go. If it doesn't, ask Intourist what you can do to get
authorization. Be sure that you receive your ticket in plenty of
time and fully understand the flight details. You should make all
necessary arrangements for accommodations prior to departure.

USEFUL WORDS AND PHRASES

aircraft	самолёт	*samalyot*
airline	авиакомпания	*aveea-kompaneeya*
airport	аэропорт	*aeraport*
arrival	прибытие	*preebiteeye*
baggage claim	выдача багажа	*vidacha bagazha*
boarding pass	посадочный талон	*pasadachni talon*
check-in (*noun*)	регистрация	*ryegeestratsee-ya*
check-in desk	стойка регистрации	*stoyka ryegeestratsee*
customs	таможня	*tamozhnya*
delay	задержка	*zadyershka*
departure	отправление	*atpravlyeneeye*
departure lounge	зал вылета	*zal vilyeta*
emergency exit	запасной выход	*zapasnoy vikhat*
fire exit	пожарный выход	*pazharni vikhat*
flight	рейс	*ryays*
flight attendant		
(*male*)	бортпроводник	*bart-pravadneek*
(*female*)	стюардесса	*styoo-ardyesa*
flight number	рейс номер	*ryays nomyer*
gate	выход на посадку	*vikhad na pasadkoo*

jet	реактивный самолёт	rye-akteevni samalyot
land (*verb*)	приземлиться	preezyemleet'sa
long-distance flight	рейс дальнего следования	ryays dal'nyeva slyeda-vanee-ya
passport	паспорт	paspart
passport control	паспортный контроль	paspartni kantrol'
pilot	пилот	peelot
runway	взлётно-посадочная полоса	vzlyotna-pasadachna-ya palasa
seat	место	myesta
seat belt	ремень	ryemyen'
takeoff (*noun*)	взлёт	vzlyot
window	окно	akno
wing	крыло	krilo

When is there a flight to …?
Когда рейс в …?
kagda ryays v …?

What time does the flight to … leave?
Когда вылетает самолёт в ...?
kagda vilyeta-yet samalyot v …?

Is it a direct flight?
Это прямой рейс?
eta pryamoy ryays?

Do I have to change planes?
Я должен (*m*)/должна (*f*) пересесть на другой самолет?
ya dolzhen/dolzhna pyeryesyest' na droogoy samalyot?

When do I have to check in?
Когда я должен (*m*)/должна (*f*) быть в аэропорту для регистрации?
kagda ya dolzhen/dolzhna bit' vaeraportoo dlya ryegeestratsee?

I'd like a one-way ticket to …
Дайте, пожалуйста, билет водин конец до ...
dIt-ye, pazhalsta beelyet vadeen konyets do …

I'd like a round-trip ticket to …
Дайте, пожалуйста, билет в оба конца до ...
dIt-ye, pazhalsta beelyet voba kantsa do …

I'd like a nonsmoking seat, please
Я хочу место в отделении для некурящих
ya khachoo myesta vatdyelyenee dlya nyekooryasheekh

I'd like a window seat, please
Я хочу место у окна, пожалуйста
ya khachoo myesta oo akna, pazhalsta

How long will the flight be delayed?
На сколько задерживается рейс?
na skol'ka zadyerzheeva-yetsa ryays?

Which gate for the flight to …?
Какой выход на посадку на рейс до ...?
kakoy vikhad na pasadkoo na ryays do …?

When do we arrive in …?
Когда мы прибываем в ...?
kagda mi preebiva-yem v …?

May I smoke now?
Теперь можно курить?
tyepyer' mozhna kooreet'?

I do not feel very well
Мне плохо
mnye plokha

THINGS YOU'LL SEE

Аэрофлот	*aeraflot*	Aeroflot
бортпроводник	*bart-pravadneek*	flight attendant (male)
выдача багажа	*vidacha bagazha*	baggage claim
вынужденная посадка	*vinoozhdyenna-ya pasadka*	emergency landing
высота	*visata*	altitude
выход на посадку	*vikhod na pasadkoo*	gate
задержка	*zadyershka*	delay
запасной выход	*zapasnoy vikhot*	emergency exit
информация	*eenformatsee-ya*	information
местное время	*myestna-ye vryemya*	local time
не курить	*nye kooreet'*	no smoking
отправление	*atpravlyeneeye*	departures
паспортный контроль	*paspartni kantrol'*	passport control
пассажиры	*pasazheeri*	passengers
пожарный выход	*pazharni vikhot*	fire exit
прибытие	*preebiteeye*	arrivals
пристегните ремни	*pree-styegneet-ye ryemnee*	fasten seat belts
прямой рейс	*pryamoy ryays*	direct flight
регистрация	*ryegeestratsee-ya*	check-in
регулярный рейс	*ryegoolyarni ryays*	scheduled flight
рейс	*ryays*	flight
самолёт	*samalyot*	aircraft
скорость	*skorast'*	speed
стюардесса	*styoo-ardyesa*	flight attendant
таможенный контроль	*tamozheni kantrol'*	customs control
транзитная посадка	*tranzeetna-ya pasadka*	intermediate stop
явиться на регистрацию	*yaveet'sa na ryegeestratsee-yoo*	check in (verb)

THINGS YOU'LL HEAR

abyavlya-yetsa pasadka na ryays …
The flight for … is now boarding

pazhalsta, prIdeet-ye na pasadkoo k vikhadoo nomyer …
Please go now to gate number …

LOCAL PUBLIC TRANSPORTATION AND TAXIS

A one-way ride on a bus, tram, or trolley costs a flat fare equivalent to no more than a few cents. One-way tickets are no longer sold on the vehicle, so get your tickets in a booklet of ten, called a книжечка (*kneezhechka*), which can be bought from the driver or at a newsstand. Validate your ticket for the ride by perforating it with one of the ticket punching machines hanging from the wall.

Bus stops have yellow signs marked "A" and trolley stops have white signs marked "T." These transportation services and the subway run from about 6 AM to about midnight. For people staying in Moscow or St. Petersburg for three or more weeks, it may be worth getting a monthly season ticket—единый (*yedeeni*)—which is valid on all forms of public transportation, including the subway. The *yedeeni*, however, is only valid for a calendar month (so from mid-January to mid-February it probably would not be worth having because you would need to buy two).

Plastic subway tokens—жетоны (*zhetoni*)—are bought from ticket offices in the station. The flat fare is relatively inexpensive compared to fares in the US. Feed a token into the slot next to the red light at the automatic barrier and you are then entitled to travel wherever you want until your ride has ended. To leave the subway, follow the выход в город (*vikhat vgorad*) signs, which mean "exit to the city."

Whenever using the subway, it is probably worth writing down the name of your destination to help identify it in Cyrillic. To change lines, look for the sign переход на поезда до станций (*pyeryekhod na pa-yezda do stantsee* ...), meaning "Change to trains for stations ...."

Available taxis can be identified by a green light in the front of the windshield. Frequently, unofficial taxi drivers will offer to pick you up. In all such cases it is wise to fix the price in advance. (If you are clearly being fleeced once you reach your destination, give no more than a reasonable maximum, forget all your Russian, and depart expressing bewilderment and indignation in English.) Treat tipping just as you would at home.

Some areas also offer ferry services. The expressions below cover all forms of public transportation, including boats.

USEFUL WORDS AND PHRASES

adult	взрослый	*vzrosli*
bus	автобус	*aftoboos*
bus stop	остановка автобуса	*astanofka aftoboosa*
child	ребёнок	*ryebyonak*
conductor	кондуктор	*kandooktar*
connection	пересадка	*pyeryesatka*
cruise	круиз	*kroo-eez*
dock	пристань	*preestan'*
driver	водитель	*vadeetyel'*
fare	стоимость проезда	*sto-eemast' pra-yezda*
ferry	паром	*parom*
lake	озеро	*ozyera*
number 5 bus	пятый автобус	*pyati aftoboos*
passenger	пассажир	*pasazheer*
river	река	*ryeka*
sea	море	*mor-ye*
seat	место	*myesta*
ship	теплоход	*tyeplakhot*
station	станция	*stantsee-ya*
subway	метро	*myetro*
taxi	такси	*taksee*
terminal	конечный пункт	*kanyechni poonkt*
ticket	билет	*beelyet*
tram	трамвай	*tramvi*
transit system map	схема	*skhyema*
underground passage	подземный переход	*padzyemni pyeryekhot*

Where is the nearest subway station?
Где ближайшая станция метро?
gdye bleezhisha-ya stantsee-ya myetro?

Where is the bus station?
Где автобусная станция?
gdye aftoboosna-ya stantsee-ya?

Where is there a bus stop?
Где остановка автобуса?
gdye astanofka aftoboosa?

Which buses go to ...?
Какие автобусы идут до ...?
kakeeye aftoboosi eedoot do ...?

How often do the buses go to ...?
Как часто ходят автобусы в ...?
kak chasta khodyat aftoboosi v ...?

Would you tell me when we get to ...?
Скажите, пожалуйста, когда мы приедем в ...?
skazheet-ye, pazhalsta, kagda mi pree-yedyem v ...?

Do I have to get off yet?
Мне пора выходить?
mnye para vikhadeet'?

How do you get to ...?
Как добраться до ...?
kak dabrat'sa do ...?

Is it very far?
Это далеко?
eta dalyeko?

I want to go to …
Я хочу поехать в …
ya khachoo pa-yekhat' v …

Do you go near …?
Вы едете в сторону …?
vi yedyet-ye fstoranoo …?

Where can I buy a ticket?
Где можно купить билет?
gdye mozhna koopeet' beelyet?

Could you close/open the window?
Закройте/откройте окно, пожалуйста?
zakroyt-ye/atkroyt-ye akno, pazhalsta?

Could you help me get a ticket?
Вы не поможете мне купить билет?
vi nye pamozhet-ye mnye koopeet' beelyet?

When does the last bus leave?
Когда отходит последний автобус?
kagda atkhodeet paasslyednee aftoboos?

THINGS YOU'LL HEAR

beelyeti, pazhalsta
Tickets, please

astarozhna, dvyeree zakriva-yootsa!
Be careful, the doors are closing!

slyedoo-yooshaa-ya stantsee-ya …
The next station is …

THINGS YOU'LL SEE

билет	*beeleyet*	ticket
взрослые	*vzrosliye*	adults
вход	*fkhot*	entrance
дети	*dyetee*	children
запасной выход	*zapasnoy vikhat*	emergency exit
конечный пункт	*kanyechni poonkt*	terminal
контролёр	*kantralyor*	ticket inspector
маршрут	*marshroot*	route
места	*myesta*	seats
мест нет	*myest nyet*	full
не курить	*nye kooreet'*	no smoking
нет входа	*nyet fkhoda*	no entrance
остановка	*astanofka*	stop
отправление	*atpravlyeneeye*	departures
пожарный выход	*pazharni vikhat*	fire exit
разговаривать	*razgavareevat'*	do not speak to
с водителем	*svadeetyelyem*	the driver
запрещается	*zapryesha-yetsa*	
стоянка такси	*sta-yanka taksee*	taxi stand

DOING BUSINESS

In addition to the usual information, your business card should state how you can be contacted from Russia. It is a good idea to have your business card and any literature about your company in both English and Russian. Owing to the chronic shortage of public telephone lines and the slowness of the postal service, you should consider establishing an alternative means of communication such as fax.

If your delegation does not have a Russian speaker, make sure in advance that the Russian side will supply qualified translators at all meetings.

It will be handy to have some gifts with you for appropriate occasions, especially gifts with obvious Western kudos such as high-tech gadgets or Scotch whiskey. Even more than in the West, the key figure to impress is the top man. He and his senior colleagues should be treated with particular attentiveness wherever possible by representatives of corresponding rank from your own company.

Clearly, personal tact and business experience best dictate how to handle personal relationships with your Russian partners. Do not insult them by arguing over payment for any hospitality they are providing. Equally, do not take for granted how attractive they find contact with Westerners. Apart from a widespread partiality for Western consumer goods, mention of future business trips to the West is, where appropriate, likely to prove a strong incentive to them to continue business relations.

USEFUL WORDS AND PHRASES

accept	принимать	*preeneemat'*
accountant	бухгалтер	*bookhgaltyer*
accounts department	бухгалтерия	*bookhgaltyeree-ya*
advertise	рекламировать	*ryeklameeravat'*
advertisement	реклама	*ryeklama*

airfreight	воздушная доставка	*vazdooshna-ya dastafka*
bid	заявка	*za-yafka*
bill (*verb*)	выставить счёт	*vistaveet' shyot*
board (*of directors*)	правление	*pravlyeneeye*
brochure	брошюра	*brashyoora*
business card	карточка (визитная)	*kartachka (veezytnaya)*
chairman	председатель	*pryedsyedatyel'*
client	клиент	*klee-yent*
company	компания	*kampanee-ya*
computer	компьютер	*kampyootyer*
consumer	потребитель	*patryebeetyel'*
contract	договор	*dagavor*
cost	стоимость	*sto-eemast'*
customer	покупатель	*pakoopatyel'*
director	директор	*deeryektar*
discount	скидка	*skeetka*
documents	документы	*dakoomyenti*
down payment	аванс	*avans*
engineer	инженер	*eenzhenyer*
executive	исполнитель	*eespalneetyel'*
expensive	дорогой	*daragoy*
exports	экспорт	*eksport*
fax	факс	*faks*
import (*verb*)	импортировать	*eemporteeravat'*
imports	импорт	*eemport*
inexpensive	дешёвый	*dyeshyovi*
installment	очередной взнос	*achyeryednoy vznos*
invoice	накладная	*nakladna-ya*
letter	письмо	*pees'mo*
letter of credit	аккредитив	*akryedeeteev*
loss	ущерб	*oosherp*
manager	управляющий	*oopravlya-yooshee*

manufacture	изготовление	*eezgatavlyeneeye*
margin	маржа	*mar-zha*
market	рынок	*rinak*
marketing	маркетинг	*markyeteen*
meeting	встреча	*fstryecha*
negotiations	переговоры	*pyeryegavori*
offer	предложение	*pryedlazheneeye*
order (*noun*)	заказ	*zakas*
order (*verb*)	заказывать	*zakazivat'*
personnel	персонал	*pyersanal*
price	цена	*tsena*
product	продукция	*pradooktsee-ya*
production	производство	*pra-eezvotstva*
profit	прибыль	*preebil'*
promotion	продвижение	*pradveezheneeye*
(*publicity*)	с помощью	*spomash'yoo*
	рекламы	*ryeklami*
purchase order	закупочный заказ	*zakoopachni zakas*
sales department	отдел продаж	*atdyel pradazh*
sales director	директор по	*deeryektar po*
	продаже	*pradazhe*
sales figures	статистика	*stateesteeka*
	продаж	*pradazh*
secretary	секретарь (*m*)	*syekryetar'*
	секретарша (*f*)	*syekryetarsha*
shipment	доставка морем	*dastafka moryem*
tax	налог	*nalok*
tender (*noun*)	тендер	*tender*
total	итог	*eetok*

My name is …
Меня зовут ...
myenya zavoot …

Here's my card
Вот моя карточка
vot ma-ya kartachka

Pleased to meet you
Рад (*m*)/рада (*f*) познакомиться
rad/rada paznakomeet'sa

May I introduce …?
Позвольте представить ...
pazvol't-ye prryedstaveet' …

My company is …
Моя компания ...
maa-ya kampanee-ya …

Our product is selling very well in the US market
Наша продукция очень хорошо продаётся на
  США рынке
*nasha pradooktsee-ya ochhyen' kharasho prada-yotsa na
  s'sha rink-ye*

We are looking for partners in Russia
Мы ищем партнёров в России
mi eeshem partnyoraf vrasee

At our last meeting …
На нашей последней встрече ...
na nashay paslyednay fstryeche …

10/25/50 percent
десять/двадцать пять/пятьдесят процентов
dyesyat'/dvatsat' pyat'/pyadyeesyat pratsentaf

More than …
Больше чем …
bol'she chyem …

Less than …
Меньше чем …
myenshe chyem …

We're on schedule
Мы сделаем в срок
mi zdelayem vsrok

We're slightly behind schedule
Мы немного отстаём от сроков
mi nyeemnoga atsta-yom atsrokaf

Please accept our apologies
Пожалуйста, примите наши извинения
pazhalsta, preemeet-ye nashee eezveenyenee-ya

There are good government grants available
Имеются хорошие правительственные дотации
eemye-yootsa kharosheeye praveetyel'stvenniye datatsee

It's a deal
Договорились
dagavareelees'

We'll send them airfreight
Мы отправим это самолетом
mi atpravim eta samolyotom

I'll have to check that with my chairman
Я должен (m)/я должна (f) обсудить это с моим
   председателем
ya dolzhen/dalzhna absoodeet'eta sma-eem pryedsyedatyelyem

I'll get back to you on that
Я обращусь к вам позже по этому вопросу
ya abrashoos' kvam pozhe po etamoo vaprosoo

You will get our quote very shortly
Наши расценки вы получите в ближайшее время
nashee rastsenkee vi paloocheet-ye vbleezhishye-ye vryemya

It's a pleasure to do business with you
Приятно иметь дело с вами
pree-yatna eemyet' dyela svamee

**We look forward to a mutually beneficial business
   relationship**
Мы ожидаем взаимовыгодного делового сотрудничества
mi azheeda-yem vza-eemavigadnava dyelavova saatroodneechyestva

RESTAURANTS

The highest standards of service and food are now undoubtedly to be found in Western-managed hotels and restaurants in the big cities. However, prices tend to be quite high, and the dishes generally more oriented toward Western cuisine than Russian.

There is now a large number of private restaurants and cafés that, in general, offer good, and in some cases excellent, standards of both cuisine and service. Prices vary and you must now pay in roubles in all restaurants. Some of the more renowned private restaurants in Moscow include "U Pirosmani" (Georgian), "Skazka," "Glazour," and "Arleccino." Expect some form of live entertainment here in the evenings, ranging from classical music to topless cabaret. The best way to keep up-to-date with the restaurant scene is to read one of the free English-language newspapers (for instance, the *Moscow Tribune* or *Guardian*), normally available in hotel lobbies.

Finally there are the state-run restaurants, where, on the whole, standards of service and cuisine have declined in recent years. Their principal attraction now is that most of them are still reasonably priced, meaning it is possible to eat a hearty meal with caviar and champagne without breaking the bank. However, these restaurants remain difficult to book, unless the restaurant in question happens to be in your hotel (as a resident you should assume that you are entitled to dine there).

To avoid disappointment it is always advisable to book your table at least one day in advance, even at the Western-managed restaurants. If you decide to book a table at a state-run restaurant, you should start to make arrangements for this well in advance. It is also worthwhile to try to get in on the weekend since this is when these establishments are at their most animated.

St. Petersburg justifiably prides itself on better culinary standards than Moscow, making the choice for the consumer wider. As in the West, restaurants' reputations fluctuate, and it is always worth asking locals for the most current recommendations on eating out.

Apart from caviar, vodka (which is ordered by the gram in restaurants), and dry champagne, strongly recommended are the пельмени (*pyelmyenee*, meat dumplings), блины (*bleeni*, pancakes), щи (*shee*, cabbage soup), борщ (*borsch*, beet and cabbage soup with beef or pork), and fresh fish. The best Soviet wines come from Georgia and the Crimea and the finest cognac is Armenian.

It is possible to eat inexpensively in more humble establishments, although the food might seem rather basic when compared to the West. The usual rule (as with Russian stores) is simply "what you see is what you get." The café—кафе (*kafe*)—is slightly more down-scale than the restaurant, and the столовая (*stalova-ya*) is similar to a canteen. Choose one that smells good and looks clean.

Instant snacks are available at a закусочная (*zakoosachna-ya*). A пельменная (*pyel'myenna-ya*) serves meat dumplings and a шашлычная (*shashlichna-ya*) serves spicy meat on a skewer.

The пивной бар (*peevnoy bar*, literally "beer bar") serves a considerable range of beers, soft and alcoholic drinks, and traditional Russian food (depending on the class). Traditional English and Irish pubs are now found as well (the most well-known and popular are John Bull and Rosie O'Grady's). The bars in the larger hotels offer a fair range of alcohol and cigarettes for consumption in surroundings that are usually fairly congenial.

USEFUL WORDS AND PHRASES

beer	пиво	*peeva*
bill	счёт	*shyot*
bottle	бутылка	*bootilka*
bowl	тарелка	*taryelka*
cake	кекс	*kyeks*
caviar	икра	*eekra*
champagne	шампанское	*shampanska-ye*
chef	повар	*povar*

coffee	кофе	_kof-ye_
cup	чашка	_chashka_
fork	вилка	_veelka_
glass	стакан	_stakan_
knife	нож	_nosh_
menu	меню	_myenyoo_
milk	молоко	_malako_
mineral water	минеральная вода	_meenyeral'na-ya vada_
napkin	салфетка	_salfyetka_
plate	тарелка	_taryelka_
receipt	чек	_chyek_
sandwich	бутерброд	_bootyerbrot_
soup	суп	_soop_
spoon	ложка	_loshka_
sugar	сахар	_sakhar_
table	стол	_stol_
tea	чай	_chI_
teaspoon	чайная ложка	_chIna-ya loshka_
tip	чаевые	_cha-yeviye_
waiter	официант	_afeetsee-ant_
waitress	официантка	_afeetsee-antka_
water	вода	_vada_
wine	вино	_veeno_

A table for two, please
Стол на двоих, пожалуйста
stol na dva-eekh, pazhalsta

But I have reserved a table
Но я заказал (_m_)/заказала (_f_) стол
no ya zakazal/zakazala stol

But those tables are free
Но эти столы свободны
no etee stali svabodni

Can I see the menu?
Можно посмотреть меню?
mozhna pasmatryet' myenyoo?

I would like to reserve a table for tomorrow evening
Я хочу заказать стол на завтрашний вечер
ya khacho zakazat' stol na zaftrashnee vyechyer

What would you recommend?
Что вы посоветуете?
shto vi pasavyetoo-yet-ye?

I'd like …
Я хочу …
ya khachoo …

100/200 grams of vodka, please
сто/двести граммов водки, пожалуйста
sto/dvyestee gramaf votkee, pazhalsta

Just a cup of coffee, please
Просто чашку кофе, пожалуйста
prosta chashkoo kof-ye, pazhalsta

Waiter!
Официант!
afeetsee-ant!

Can we have the bill, please?
Счёт, пожалуйста
shyot, pazhalsta

I only want a snack
Я хочу только закуску
ya khachoo tol'ka zakooskoo

I didn't order this
Я не заказывал (m)/заказывала (f) это
ya nye zakazival/zakazivala eta

May we have some more …?
Можно ещё …?
mozhna yeshyo …?

The meal was very good, thank you
Спасибо, было очень вкусно
spaseeba, bila ochyen' fkoosna

THINGS YOU'LL HEAR

pree-yatnava apyeteeta
Enjoy your meal

MENU GUIDE

APPETIZERS

блины с икрой (*bleeni seekroy*) — pancakes with caviar

блины со сметаной (*bleeni sa smyetanay*) — pancakes with sour cream

грибы в сметане (*greebi fsmyetan-ye*) — mushrooms in sour cream

грибы маринованые (*greebi mareenovaniye*) — marinated mushrooms

закуски (*zakooskee*) — appetizers

заливная рыба (*zaleevna-ya riba*) — fish in aspic

икра (*eekra*) — caviar

икра баклажанная (*eekra baklazhana-ya*) — eggplant with onions and tomatoes

икра зернистая (*eekra zyerneesta-ya*) — fresh caviar

икра кетовая (*eekra kyetova-ya*) — red caviar

кильки (*keel'kee*) — sprats (herring)

лососина (*lasaseena*) — salmon

осетрина заливная (*asyetreena zaleevna-ya*) — sturgeon in aspic

осетрина с гарниром (*asyetreena zgarneeram*) — sturgeon with garnish

сардины в масле (*sardeeni vmasl-ye*) — sardines in oil

сёмга (*syomga*) — salmon

солёные огурцы (*salyoniye agoortsi*) — pickled cucumbers

солёные помидоры (*salyoniye pameedori*) — pickled tomatoes

фаршированные помидоры (*farsheerovaniye pameedori*) — stuffed tomatoes

SOUPS

борщ (*borsh*) — beet and cabbage soup with beef or pork

бульон с пирожками (*bool'yon speerashkamee*) — clear soup with small meat pies

бульон с фрикадельками (*bool'yon sfreekadyel'kamee*) — clear soup with meatballs

мясной бульон (*myasnoy bool'yon*) — clear meat soup

овощной суп (*avashnoy soop*) — vegetable soup

окрошка (*akroshka*) — cold summer soup

рассольник (*rasol'neek*) — pickled cucumber soup

MENU GUIDE

солянка (*sal<u>ya</u>nka*) — spicy soup made from fish or meat and vegetables

суп из свежих грибов (*soop eez sv<u>ye</u>zheekh greeb<u>o</u>f*) — fresh mushroom soup

суп картофельный (*soop kart<u>o</u>fyel'ni*) — potato soup

суп-лапша с курицей (*soop l<u>a</u>psha sk<u>oo</u>reetsay*) — chicken noodle soup

суп мясной (*soop myasn<u>o</u>y*) — meat soup

суп томатный (*soop tam<u>a</u>tni*) — tomato soup

уха (<u>oo</u>kha) — fish soup

харчо (*kharch<u>o</u>*) — thick, spicy mutton soup from Georgia

щи (*shee*) — cabbage soup

Egg Dishes

омлет натуральный (*aml<u>ye</u>t nat<u>oo</u>ral'ni*) — plain omelette

омлет с ветчиной (*aml<u>ye</u>t svyetch<u>ee</u>noy*) — ham omelette

яичница-глазунья (*ya-<u>ee</u>chneetsa glaz<u>oo</u>n'ya*) — fried eggs

яйца вкрутую (*y<u>ltsa fkrootoo</u>-yoo*) — hard-boiled eggs

яйца всмятку (*y<u>l</u>tsa fsm<u>ya</u>tkoo*) — soft-boiled eggs

яйцо (*y<u>l</u>tso*) — egg

яйцо под майонезом (*y<u>l</u>tso pod mlany<u>e</u>zam*) — mayonnaise

Fish

ассорти рыбное (*asart<u>ee</u> r<u>i</u>bna-ye*) — assorted fish

жареная рыба (*zh<u>a</u>ryena-ya r<u>i</u>ba*) — fried fish

камбала (*k<u>a</u>mbala*) — plaice

карп с грибами (*karp zgreeb<u>a</u>mee*) — carp with mushrooms

кета (*ky<u>e</u>ta*) — Siberian salmon

копчёная сёмга (*kapch<u>yo</u>na-ya s<u>yo</u>mga*) — smoked salmon

осетрина под белым соусом (*asyetr<u>ee</u>na pod by<u>e</u>lim s<u>o</u>-oosam*) — sturgeon in white sauce

осетрина с гарниром (*asyetr<u>ee</u>na zgarn<u>ee</u>ram*) — sturgeon with garnish

осетрина с пикантным соусом (*asyetr<u>ee</u>na speek<u>a</u>ntnim s<u>o</u>-oosam*) — sturgeon in piquant sauce

осётр, запечённый в сметане (*as<u>yo</u>tr zapyech<u>yo</u>ni fsmyet<u>a</u>n-ye*) — sturgeon baked in sour cream

палтус (*p<u>a</u>ltoos*) — halibut

печень трески в масле
  (*pyechyen' tryeskee vmasl-ye*)

cod liver in oil

рыбные блюда (*ribniye blyooda*)

fish dishes

сельдь (*sye'ld'*)

herring

селёдка малосольная
  (*syelyodka malasol'na-ya*)

slightly salted herring

скумбрия запечённая
  (*skoombree-ya zapyechyona-ya*)

baked mackerel

судак в белом вине (*soodak vbyelam veen-ye*)

pike perch in white wine

судак, жаренный в тесте
  (*soodak zharyeni ftyest-ye*)

pike perch fried in batter

судак по-русски (*soodak pa-rooskee*)

pike perch Russian style

треска (*tryeska*)

cod

тунец (*toonyets*)

tuna fish

фаршированная рыба (*farsheerovana-ya riba*)

stuffed fish

форель (*faryel'*)

trout

шпроты (*shproti*)

sprats (*herring*)

щука (*shooka*)

pike

MEAT DISHES

азу (*azoo*)

small pieces of meat in a savory sauce

ассорти мясное (*asartee myasno-ye*)

assorted meats

тефтели (*tyeftyelee*)

meatballs

голубцы (*galooptsee*)

cabbage leaves stuffed with meat and rice

дичь (*deech*)

game

колбаса (*kalbasa*)

salami sausage, or boiled sausage

копчёная колбаса (*kapchyona-ya kalbasa*)

smoked sausage

мясо (*myasa*)

meat

печёнка (*pyechyonka*)

liver

почки (*pochkee*)

kidneys

рубленое мясо (*rooblyena-ye myasa*)

ground meat

рубленые котлеты (*rooblyeniye katlyeti*)

type of meatball

сосиски (*saseeskee*)

hot dogs

студень (*stoodyen'*)

aspic

тефтели с рисом (*tyeftyelee sreesam*)

small meatballs with rice

филе (*filyay*)

fillet

шашлык (*shashlik*)

kebab

MENU GUIDE

BEEF

антрекот (*antryekot*)   entrecote steak
беф-строганов (*byef-stroganaf*)   beef Stroganoff
бифштекс натуральный   fried or grilled beefsteak
    (*beefshtyeks natooral'ni*)
говядина отварная с хреном   boiled beef with
    (*gavyadeena atvarna-ya skhryenam*)   horseradish
говядина тушёная (*gavyadeena tooshyona-ya*)   stewed beef
гуляш из говядины (*goolyush eez gavyadeeni*)   beef goulash
котлеты с грибами (*katlyeti zgreebamee*)   steak with mushrooms
рагу из говядины (*ragoo eez gavyadeeni*)   beef ragout
ромштекс с луком (*romshtyeks slookam*)   steak with onion
ростбиф с гарниром (*rostbeef zgarneeram*)   cold roast beef with garnish

LAMB

баранина (*baraneena*)   mutton, lamb
бараньи отбивные (*baran'ee atbeevniye*)   lamb chops
баранина на вертеле (*baraneena na vyertyel-ye*)   mutton grilled on a skewer
битки из баранины (*beetkee eez baraninee*)   lamb steaks
рагу из баранины (*ragoo eez baraneeni*)   lamb ragout
шашлык из баранины (*shashlik eez baraneeni*)   lamb kebab

PORK

буженина с гарниром   cold boiled pork with garnish
    (*boozheneena zgarneeram*)
ветчина (*vyetchina*)   ham
картофель с ветчиной и шпиком   potatoes with ham and
    (*kartofyel' zvyetchinay ee shpeekam*)   bacon fat
копчёные свиные рёбрышки с фасолью   smoked pork ribs with
    (*kapchoniye sveeniye ryobrishkee sfasol'yoo*)   beans
окорок (*okarak*)   hamsteaks
свинина жареная с гарниром   fried pork with garnish
    (*sveeneena zharyena-ya zgarneeram*)
свинина с квашеной капустой   pork with sauerkraut
    (*sveeneena skvashenay kapoostay*)

свиные отбивные с чесноком   pork chops with garlic
   (*sveeniye atbeevniye schesnakom*)
шашлык из свинины с рисом   pork kebab with rice
   (*shashlik eez sveeneeni sreesam*)

VEAL

битки (*beetkee*)   steaks or ground steak
рулет из рубленой телятины   ground veal roll
   (*roolyet eez rooblyenay tyelyateeni*)
телятина (*tyelyateena*)   veal
телячьи отбивные (*tyelyach'ee atbeevni-ye*)   veal chops
фрикадели из телятины в соусе   veal meatballs in gravy
   (*freekadyelee eez tyelyateeni vso-oos-ye*)
шницель с яичницей-глазуньей   schnitzel with fried egg
   (*shneetsyel' sya-eechneetsay glazoon'yay*)

POULTRY

блюда из птицы (*blyooda eez pteetsi*)   poultry dishes
гусь жареный с капустой или яблоками   roast goose with cabbage
   (*goos' zharyeni skapoostay eelee yablakamee*)   or apples
индейка (*indyayka*)   turkey
котлеты по-киевски (*katlyeti pa-kee-yefskee*)   chicken Kiev
пожарские котлеты (*pazharskiye katlyeti*)   ground chicken
курица (*kooreetsa*)   chicken
отварной цыплёнок (*atvarnoy tsiplyonak*)   boiled chicken
панированный цыпленок   chicken in bread crumbs
   (*paneerovani tsiplyonak*)
птица (*pteetsa*)   poultry
утка (*ootka*)   duck
цыплёнок в тесте (*tsiplyonak ftyest-ye*)   chicken in pastry
цыплёнок по-охотничьи   chicken with white wine sauce
   (*tsiplyonak pa-akhotneechee*)   and mushrooms
цыплёнок «табака» (*tsiplyonak tabaka*)   Caucasian chicken with
        garlic sauce
цыплёнок фрикасе (*tsiplyonak freekasye*)   chicken fricassee
чахохбили (*chakhokhbeelee*)   chicken casserole Georgian style

PIES AND PASTRY DISHES

изделия из теста (*eezdyelee-ya eez tyesta*)	pastry dishes
пельмени (*pyel'myenee*)	meat dumplings
пирог (*peerok*)	pie
пирожки (*peerashkee*)	pies
пирожки с капустой (*peerashkee skapoostay*)	pies filled with cabbage
пирожки с мясом (*peerashkee smyasam*)	pies filled with meat
пирожки с творогом (*peerashkee stvoragam*)	pies filled with cottage cheese
тесто (*tyesta*)	pastry

VEGETABLES

баклажан (*baklazhan*)	eggplant
жареный картофель (*zharyeni kartofyel'*)	fried potatoes
зелёный горошек (*zyelyoni garoshek*)	green peas
кабачки (*kabachkee*)	zucchini
капуста (*kapoosta*)	cabbage
картофель (*kartofyel'*)	potatoes
кислая капуста (*keesla-ya kapoosta*)	sauerkraut
лук (*look*)	onions, scallions
морковь (*markof'*)	carrots
овощи (*ovashchee*)	vegetables
огурец (*agooryets*)	cucumber
перец (*pyeryets*)	pepper
петрушка (*pyetrooshka*)	parsley
помидоры (*pameedori*)	tomatoes
с гарниром (*zgarneeram*)	with garnish
свёкла (*svyokla*)	beets
фасоль (*fasol'*)	French, haricot, or kidney beans
цветная капуста (*tsvyetna-ya kapoosta*)	cauliflower
чеснок (*chyesnok*)	garlic

SALADS

винегрет (*veenyegryet*)	vegetable salad
зелёный салат (*zyelyoni salat*)	green salad
огурцы со сметаной (*agoortsi sa smyetanay*)	cucumber in sour cream
салат «Здоровье» (*salat zdarov'ye*)	"health" salad, mixed vegetable salad
салат из лука (*salat eez looka*)	scallion salad

салат из огурцов (sal*a*t eez agoorts*of*)   cucumber salad
салат из помидоров (sal*a*t eez pameed*o*raf)   tomato salad
салат из помидоров с брынзой   tomato salad with goat cheese
  (sal*a*t eez pameed*o*raf zbr*i*nzay)
салат из редиски (sal*a*t eez ryed*ee*skee)   radish salad
салат мясной (sal*a*t myasn*oy*)   meat salad
салат с крабами (sal*a*t skr*a*bamee)   crab salad

Pasta and Rice

вермишель (vyermeesh*e*l')   vermicelli
лапша (lapsh*a*)   noodles
макароны (makar*o*ni)   macaroni
плов (pl*o*f)   pilaf
рис (rees)   rice

Bread

баранки (bar*a*nkee)   ring-shaped rolls
белый хлеб (b*ye*li khlyep)   white bread
бородинский хлеб (barad*ee*nskee khlyep)   black rye bread
булки (b*oo*lkee)   rolls
бутерброд с сыром (bootyerbr*o*t s-s*i*ram)   cheese sandwich
ржаной хлеб (rzhan*oy* khlyep)   black rye bread
хлеб (khlyep)   bread
чёрный хлеб (ch*yo*rni khlyep)   brown bread

Cakes and Desserts

блинчики с вареньем   pancakes with jam
  (bl*ee*ncheekee svar*ye*n'yem)
блины (bl*ee*ni)   pancakes
блины со сметаной (bl*ee*ni sa smyet*a*nay)   pancakes with sour cream
вареники (var*ye*neeki)   curd or fruit dumplings
ватрушка (vatr*oo*shka)   cheesecake
галушки (gal*oo*shki)   dumplings
десерт (dyes*ye*rt)   dessert
желе (zhely*ay*)   gelatin
кекс (kyeks)   fruit cake
кисель (kis*ye*l')   thin fruit gelatin
кисель из клубники (kees*ye*l' eez kloobn*ee*kee)   strawberry gelatin

кисель из чёрной смордины
(*keesyel' eez chyornoy smarodeeni*)
black currant gelatin

компот из груш (*kampot eez groosh*)
stewed pears

компот из сухофруктов
(*kampot eez sookha-frooktaf*)
stewed dried fruit
  mixture

конфета (*kanfyeta*)
candy

коржик (*korzheek*)
flat dry shortbread

крем (*kryem*)
butter cake filling

молочный кисель (*malochni keesyel'*)
milk gelatin

мороженое клубничное
(*marozhena-ye kloobneechna-ye*)
strawberry ice cream

мороженое молочное
(*marozhena-ye malochna-ye*)
ice cream

мороженое молочное с ванилином
(*marozhena-yemalochna-ye svaneeleenam*)
vanilla ice cream

мороженое «пломбир»
(*marozhena-ye plambeer*)
ice cream with candied fruit

мороженое шоколадное
(*marozhena-ye shakaladna-ye*)
chocolate ice cream

печенье (*pyechyen'ye*)
cookies

пирог с повидлом (*peerok spadleevam*)
pie with jam

пирог с яблоками (*peerok syablakamee*)
apple pie

пирожное (*peerozhna-ye*)
small cake

повидло (*paveedla*)
thick gelatin

пончики (*poncheekee*)
doughnuts

салат из яблок (*salat eez yablak*)
apple salad

сдобное тесто (*zdobna-ye tyesta*)
sweet pastry

сладкое (*sladka-ye*)
dessert, sweet course

сырники (*sirneekee*)
cheesecakes

торт (*tort*)
cake, gateau

фруктовое мороженое
(*frooktova-yemarozhena-ye*)
fruit ice cream

шоколад (*shakalat*)
chocolate

эскимо (*eskeemo*)
chocolate-covered ice cream bar

CHEESE

брынза (*brinza*)
goat cheese, feta

плавленый сыр (*plavlyeni sir*)
processed cheese

сыр (*sir*)
cheese

творог (*tvorog*)
cottage cheese

FRUITS AND NUTS

абрикосы (*abreekosi*)	apricots
апельсины (*apyel'seeni*)	oranges
арбуз (*arboos*)	watermelon
банан (*banan*)	banana
виноград (*veenagrat*)	grapes
грецкий орех (*gryetskee aryekh*)	walnut
груши (*grooshee*)	pears
дыня (*dinya*)	melon
клубника (*kloobneeka*)	strawberries
лимон (*leemon*)	lemon
малина (*maleena*)	raspberries
мандарины (*mandareeni*)	mandarin oranges
орехи (*aryekhee*)	nuts
персик (*pyerseek*)	peach
сливы (*sleevi*)	plums
фрукты (*frookti*)	fruit
черешня (*cheryeshnya*)	cherries
чёрная смородина (*chyorna-ya smarodeena*)	black currant
яблоки (*yablakee*)	apples

DRINKS

апельсиновый сок (*apyel'seenavi sok*)	orange juice
белое вино (*byela-ye veeno*)	white wine
вода (*vada*)	water
водка (*vodka*)	vodka
газированная вода (*gazeerovana-ya vada*)	soda water
игристое вино (*eegreesto-ye veeno*)	sparkling wine
квас (*kvas*)	kvas (nonalcoholic, carbonated drink made of fermented bread and water)
кефир (*kyefeeyr*)	kefir (sour yogurt drink)
коньяк (*kon'yak*)	brandy
кофе с молоком (*kof-ye smalakom*)	coffee with milk
красное вино (*krasna-ye veeno*)	red wine
минеральная вода (*meenyeral'na-ya vada*)	mineral water
молоко (*malako*)	milk
напитки (*napeetkee*)	drinks
перцовка (*pyertsovka*)	pepper vodka

MENU GUIDE

пиво (_peeva_)	beer
десертное вино (_dyesyertnoye veeno_)	dessert wine
томатный сок (_tamatni sok_)	tomato juice
чай (_chI_)	tea
чай с лимоном (_chI sleemonam_)	lemon tea
чёрный кофе (_chyorni kof-ye_)	black coffee
шампанское (_shampanska-ye_)	champagne
яблочный сок (_yablachni sok_)	apple juice

BASIC FOODS

варенье (_varyen'ye_)	jam, preserves
горчица (_garcheetsa_)	mustard
гренки (_gryenkee_)	croutons
гречка (_gryechka_)	buckwheat
джем (_dzhem_)	jam
каша (_kasha_)	porridge
маргарин (_margareen_)	margarine
масло (_masla_)	butter, oil
мёд (_myot_)	honey
рассол (_rasol_)	pickle
сливки (_sleefkee_)	cream
сливочное масло (_sleevachna-ye masla_)	butter
сметана (_smyetana_)	sour cream
солёное печенье (_salyona-ye pyechyen'ye_)	cracker
соль (_sol'_)	salt
соус майонез (_so-oos mIanyes_)	mayonnaise sauce
соус хрен (_so-oos khryen_)	horseradish sauce
чёрный перец (_chorni pyeryets_)	black pepper
уксус (_ooksoos_)	vinegar

CULINARY METHODS OF PREPARATION

домашний (*damashnee*)	homemade
жареный (*zharyeni*)	broiled, fried, or roasted
жаренный на вертеле (*zharyeni na vyertyel-ye*)	broiled on a skewer
отварной (*atvarnoy*)	boiled, poached
печёный (*pyechyoni*)	baked
сырой (*siroy*)	raw
тушёный (*tooshyoni*)	stewed
фаршированный (*farsheerovani*)	stuffed

MENU TERMS

блюдо (*blyooda*)	dish, course
меню (*myenyoo*)	menu
национальные русские блюда (*natseeanal'niye rooskeeye blyooda*)	Russian national dishes
горячее (*garyachyeye*)	main course
первое блюдо (*pyerva-ye blyoodo*)	first course
русская кухня (*rooska-ya kookhnya*)	Russian cuisine
фирменные блюда (*feermyeniye blooda*)	specialty dishes

SHOPPING

If you are looking for presents to take home, then one option is to visit a Берёзка (*beryozka*) store, which sells mostly souvenirs, alcohol, and tobacco. The most attractive goods are blue and white Gzhel dishes, hand-painted trays, lacquered miniature boxes and brooches from Palekh, "matryoshka" dolls, jewelry, and pretty head-scarves. Payment in these stores, as in all others, can be made only in roubles. Your hard currency can be easily changed at any of the numerous exchange offices, some of which are located in the stores themselves.

By far the widest selection of traditional Russian souvenirs and the best bargains are to be found in street art markets such as the one on the Арбат (*arbat*), or at Вернисаж (*vyerneesazh*) in Moscow. Quality and prices vary, but bargaining is an acceptable practice here. It is not recommended that food such as caviar be bought here since it may not always be the genuine article.

Two shopping malls well worth a visit are ГУМ (*goom*; the letters stand for "State Universal Shop"), opposite the Kremlin, and Петровский Пассаж (*petrovskee passazh*), just a couple of minutes' walk from the Bolshoi Theater.

Another store that should not be left off your itinerary is the "Елисеевский" (*yeleesye-evskee*) grocery store on Moscow's Tverskaya Street and its twin on St. Petersburg's Nevsky Prospekt. Despite being rather neglected by time, both stores remain striking examples of Russia's prerevolutionary style.

More ambitious shoppers may be delighted to discover that works of art and antiques are sometimes sold very unceremoniously and at relatively low prices. Before you buy, make inquiries to insure that you will not be disappointed, since without a receipt from a *beryozka* or official permission from the Ministry of Culture to take any "work of art" out of the country there is a risk that the item will be confiscated from you at the airport.

USEFUL WORDS AND PHRASES

baker	булочная	_boo_lachna-ya
bookstore	книжный магазин	_kneezh_ni maga_zeen_
bookstore	букинистический	bookeenee_steech_y-
(*secondhand*)	магазин	eskee maga_zeen_
butcher	мясо	m_ya_sa
	(*literally meat*)	
buy	купить	koo_peet'_
cash register	касса	_ka_sa
department store	универмаг	ooneevyer_mag_
drugstore	аптека	ap_tye_ka
fashion	мода	_mo_da
fishmonger	рыба	_ri_ba
	(*literally fish*)	
florist	цветы	tsvye_ti_
	(*literally flowers*)	
grocery store	бакалея	bakal_ye_-ya
	(*literally groceries*)	
inexpensive	дешёвый (*m*)	dyesh_yo_vi
	дешёвая (*f*)	dyesh_yo_va-ya
	дешёвое (*n*)	dyesh_yo_va-ye
ladies' wear	женская одежда	_zhen_ska-ya ad_ye_zhda
market	рынок	_ri_nak
menswear	мужская одежда	_moo_shska-ya
		ad_ye_zhda
newsstand	газетный киоск	ga_zye_tni kee-_osk_
pastry shop	кондитерская	kan_dee_tyerska-ya
receipt	чек	chyek
record store	грампластинки	gramplas_teen_kee
	(*literally records*)	
shoe repairer's	ремонт обуви	rye_mont_ _o_boovee
shoe store	обувь	_oboof'_
	(*literally footwear*)	
go shopping	ходить по	kha_deet'_ po
	магазинам	moga_zee_nam

souvenir store	сувениры	*soovyeneeri*
	(*literally souvenirs*)	
spend	тратить	*trateet'*
stationery store	канцтовары	*kantstavari*
store	магазин	*magazeen*
supermarket	универсам	*ooneevyersam*
toy store	игрушки	*eegrooshkee*
	(*literally toys*)	

I'd like …
Я хочу ...
ya khachoo …

Do you have …?
У вас есть ...?
oo vas yest' …?

How much is this?
Сколько это стоит?
skol'ka eta stoeet?

Where is the … department?
Где отдел ...?
gd-ye atdyel …?

Do you have any more of these?
У вас есть ещё?
oo vas yest' yeshyo?

I'd like to change this, please
Будьте добры, я хочу это поменять
bood't-ye dabri, ya khachoo eta pamyenyat'

Do you have anything less expensive?
У вас есть что-нибудь дешевле?
oo vas yest' shto-neeboot' dyeshevl-ye?

Do you have anything larger?
У вас есть побольше?
oo vas yest' pabol'shye?

Do you have anything smaller?
У вас есть поменьше?
oo vos yest' pamyen'shye?

Do you have it in other colors?
У вас есть другого цвета?
oo vas yest' droogova tsvyeta?

Could you wrap it for me, please?
Заверните, пожалуйста
zavyerneet-ye, pazhalsta

May I have a receipt?
Дайте, пожалуйста, чек
dIt-ye, pazhalsta chyek

May I have a bag, please?
Дайте, пожалуйста, пакет
dIt-ye, pazhalsta pakyet

May I try it (them) on?
Можно померять?
mozhna pamyeryat'?

Where do I pay?
где платить?
gdye plateet'?

Could I have a refund?
Я хочу получить обратно деньги
ya khachoo paloocheet' abratna dyen'gee

I'm just looking
Я просто смотрю
ya prosta smatryoo

I'll come back later
Я вернусь позже
ya vyernoos' pozhe

THINGS YOU'LL SEE

бакалея	*bakalye-ya*	groceries
букинистический магазин	*bookeeneesteechy-eskee magazeen*	secondhand bookstore
булочная	*boolachna-ya*	bakery
бытовая химия	*bitova-ya kheemee-ya*	household cleaning materials
верхний этаж	*vyerkhnee etash*	upper floor
возьмите тележку/ корзину	*vazmeet-ye tyelyeshkoo/ karzeenoo*	please take a cart/basket
женская одежда	*zhenska-ya adyezhda*	ladies' clothing
игрушки	*eegrooshkee*	toys
канцтовары	*kantstavari*	stationery store
касса	*kasa*	cash register
книги	*kneegee*	bookstore
количество	*kaleechyestva*	quantity
кондитерская	*kandeetyerska-ya*	pastry shop
меха	*myekha*	fur store
мода	*moda*	fashion
мороженое	*marozhena-ye*	ice cream shop

→

мужская одежда	*mooshska-ya adyezhda*	menswear
мясо	*myasa*	butcher
не трогать	*nye trogat'*	please do not touch
обувь	*oboof'*	shoe store
овощи	*ovashee*	vegetables
отдел	*atdyel*	department
первый этаж	*pyervi etash*	ground floor
прокат	*prakat*	rental
самообслужи-вание	*samo-obsloozhee-vaneeye*	self-service
табак	*tabak*	tobacconist
универмаг	*ooneevyermag*	department store
цветы	*tsvyeti*	flowers
цена	*tsyena*	price

THINGS YOU'LL HEAR

oo vas yest' myelach?
Do you have anything smaller? (money)

eezveeneet-ye oo nas etava paka nyet
We're out of stock

eta vsyo, shto oo nas yest'
This is all we have

shto-neeboot' yeshyo?
Will there be anything else?

AT THE HAIRDRESSER'S

appointment	запись	*zapees'*
bangs	чёлка	*chyolka*
beard	борода	*barada*
blond (*man*)	блондин	*blandeen*
(*woman*)	блондинка	*blandeenka*
brush	щётка	*shyotka*
comb	расчёска	*raschyoska*
curlers	бигуди	*beegoodee*
curly	кудрявый	*koodryavi*
dark	тёмный	*tyomni*
gel	гель для волос	*gyel dlya valos*
hair	волосы	*volasi*
haircut	стрижка	*streeshka*
hairdresser	парикмахер	*pareekhmakhyer*
hair dryer	фен	*fyen*
hair spray	лак для волос	*lak dlya valos*
long hair	длинные волосы	*dleeniye volasi*
moustache	усы	*oosi*
part	пробор	*prabor*
perm	перманент	*pyermanyent*
shampoo	шампунь	*shampoon'*
shaving cream	крем для бритья	*kryem dlya breet'ya*
short hair	короткие волосы	*karotkeeye volasi*
wavy hair	вьющиеся волосы	*v'yooshee-yesa volasi*

I'd like to make an appointment
Я хочу записаться
ya khachoo zapeesat'sa

Just a trim, please
Немного подстигите, пожалуйста
nyemnoga padstreegeet-ye, pazhalsta

Not too much off
Много не снимайте
mnoga nye sneemIt-ye

A bit more off here, please
Покороче здесь, пожалуйста
pakaroch-ye zdyes', pazhalsta

I'd like a cut and blow-dry
Подстригите и сделайте укладку феном
padstreegeet-ye ee zdyelIt-ye ooklatkoo fyenam

I'd like a perm
Я хочу перманент
ya khachoo pyermanyent

I don't want any hair spray
Лака не нужно
laka nye noozhna

THINGS YOU'LL SEE

женский зал	*zhenskee zal*	ladies' salon
краска для волос	*kraska dlya valos*	tint
мастер	*mastyer*	hairdresser
мужской зал	*mooshskoy zal*	men's hairdresser
парикмахер	*pareekhmakhyer*	hairdresser
парикмахерская	*pareekmakherska-ya*	hairdresser's
перманент	*pyermanyent*	perm
сухой	*sookhoy*	dry
укладка	*ooklatka*	set
уложить волосы	*oolazheet' volasi*	blow dry (verb)
феном	*fyenam*	

THINGS YOU'LL HEAR

shto vi khateet-ye?
How would you like it?

eta dastatachna koratka?
Is that short enough?

pakrit' lakam?
Would you like any hair spray?

SPORTS

Active involvement in sports by tourists in Russia is most likely to mean swimming, skating, or skiing. Ask your hotel information service for specific details of how and where to do what you want. Cross-country skiing is popular, and skis for this may be rented (e.g., at Sokolneekee Park in Moscow) or even bought with relative ease. If you go anywhere off the beaten path, make sure that you are with local people who know what they are doing. Downhill skiing is becoming a popular tourist attraction in the Caucacus, but skiers should not expect it to be like Vail or Aspen. You should check well in advance with the tour organizer about what you may need to bring yourself, rather than assume that skiing equipment will be available on site.

The Black Sea resorts are excellent for swimming, and swimming pools can be found in Moscow, St. Petersburg, and the larger towns.

Full details of current sporting events for spectators can be obtained by asking your hotel information desk or Intourist. Sportsmen and women undertaking any activity outdoors in a Russian winter should be very wary of the cold—it can be ferocious.

USEFUL WORDS AND PHRASES

athletics	атлетика	*atlyeteeka*
badminton	бадминтон	*badmeenton*
ball	мяч	*myach*
beach	пляж	*plyash*
beach umbrella	солнечный зонт	*solnyechni zont*
bicycle	велосипед	*vyelaseepyet*
canoe	каноэ	*kanoe*
chess	шахматы	*shakhmati*
cross-country skiing	лыжный спорт	*lizhni sport*
cross-country skis	лыжи	*lizhee*

deck chair	шезлонг	*shezlonk*
downhill skiing	горнолыжный спорт	*garna-lizhni sport*
downhill skis	горные лыжи	*gorniye lizhee*
fishing	рыболовство	*ribalofstva*
fishing rod	удочка	*oodachka*
flippers	ласты	*lasti*
goggles	защитные очки	*zashcetniye achkee*
gymnastics	гимнастика	*geemnasteeka*
harpoon	гарпун	*garpoon*
hockey	хоккей	*khakkay*
jogging	бег трусцой	*byeg troostsoy*
lake	озеро	*ozyera*
lifeguard	спасатель	*spasatyel'*
life preserver	спасательный жилет	*spasatyel'ni zheelyet*
mountaineering	альпинизм	*al'peeneezm*
oxygen bottles	кислородные баллоны	*keeslarodniye baloni*
pedal boat	водный велосипед	*vodni vyelaseepyet*
racket	ракетка	*rakyetka*
riding	верховая езда	*vyerkhava-ya yezda*
rowboat	весельная лодка	*vyosyel'na-ya lotka*
run (*verb*)	бегать	*byegat'*
sailing	парусный спорт	*paroosni sport*
sand	песок	*pyesok*
sea	море	*mor-ye*
skate (*verb*)	кататься на коньках	*katatsa na kan'kakh*
skates	коньки	*kan'kee*
skating rink	каток	*katok*
ski (*verb*)	кататься на лыжах	*katatsa na lizhakh*
skin diving	подводное плавание	*padvodna-ye plavaneeye*
soccer	футбол	*footbol*

soccer ball	футбольный мяч	*footbol'ni myach*
soccer match	футбольный матч	*footbol'ni match*
stadium	стадион	*stadee-on*
swim *(verb)*	плавать	*plavat'*
swimming pool	бассейн	*basyeyn*
table tennis	настольный теннис	*nastolni tyenees*
tennis	теннис	*tyenees*
tennis court	теннисный корт	*tyeneesni kort*
tennis racket	теннисная ракетка	*tyeneesna-ya rakyetka*
volleyball	волейбол	*valyaybol*
walking	ходьба	*khad'ba*
water skiing	воднолыжный спорт	*vadna-lizhni sport*
water skis	водные лыжи	*vodniye lizhee*
wave	волна	*valna*
wet suit	плавательный костюм	*plavatyel'ni kastyoom*
windsurfing board	доска для сёрфинга	*daska dlya syerfeenga*
yacht	яхта	*yakhta*

How do I get to the beach?
Как попасть на пляж?
kak papast' na plyash?

How deep is the water here?
Какая глубина воды здесь?
kaka-ya gloobeena vadi zdyes'?

Is there an outdoor pool here?
Здесь есть открытый бассейн?
zdyes' yest' atkriti basyeyn?

Can I swim here?
Здесь можно плавать?
zdyes' mozhna plavat'?

Can I fish here?
Здесь можно ловить рыбу?
zdyes' mozhna laveet' riby?

Do I need a license?
Мне нужно разрешение?
mnye noozhna razryesheneeye?

I would like to rent a beach umbrella
Можно взять напрокат зонтик
mozhna vzyat' naprakat zonteek

How much does it cost per hour?
Сколько это стоит в час?
skol'ka eta sto-eet fchas?

I would like to take waterskiing lessons
Я хочу брать уроки по водным лыжам
ya khachoo brat' oorokee pa vodnim lizham

Where can I rent …?
Где можно взять напрокат ...?
gdye mozhno vsyat' naprakat …?

THINGS YOU'LL SEE

билеты	*beelyeti*	tickets
велосипедная трасса	*vyelaseepyedna-ya trasa*	bicycle path
велосипеды	*vyelaseepyedi*	bicycles
водные виды спорта	*vodniye veedi sporta*	water sports
горные лыжи	*gorniye lizhee*	downhill skis
коньки	*kan'kee*	skates
лыжи	*lizhee*	cross-country skis
напрокат	*naprakat*	for rent
не нырять	*nye niryat'*	no diving
парусные лодки	*paroosniye lotkee*	sailboats
первая помощь	*pyerva-ya pomash'*	first aid
плавать запрещается	*plavat' zapryesha-yetsa*	no swimming
пляж	*plyazh*	beach
порт	*port*	port
рыбная ловля запрещена	*ribna-ya lovlya zapryeshyena*	no fishing
спортивное оборудование	*sparteevna-ye abaroodeevaneeye*	sports facilities
спортивный центр	*sparteevni tsyentr*	sports center
спасательный жилет	*spasatyel'ni zheelyet*	life preserver
спасатель	*spasatel'*	lifeguard
стадион	*stadee-on*	stadium
уроки по водным лыжам	*oorokee pa vodnim lizham*	waterskiing lessons
футбольное поле	*footbol'na-ye pol-ye*	soccer field

POST OFFICES AND BANKS

As far as postage is concerned, it is easier to use the facilities at your hotel, if these are available, than to go to a post office. You will thus avoid long lines and be able to deal with people who are used to foreigners. You will not have to suffer the more exasperating features of the postal service, such as arbitrary closings or having no stamps. For airmail letters use a международный конверт (*mezhdoonarodni kanvyert*), or international envelope, and allow an average of two weeks for arrival. Postcards, stamps, and envelopes can be purchased at newsstands and post offices. Mailboxes are blue; in Moscow, those painted red are for local (city) mail only.

Most large towns and cities now boast a multitude of foreign exchange offices and banks where you can change hard currency for roubles and vice versa—rates do not usually vary sufficiently from bank to bank to merit shopping around. In recent years the rouble has become much more stable, eliminating the black market in currency.

Although customs currency checks have relaxed in recent years, it is still advisable to get and retain exchange receipts. These will account for expenditures of the currency you declared on your currency declaration form when you entered the country.

It should be noted that the rouble is now the only legal form of tender in Russian stores and restaurants. Hard currency is no longer accepted in its cash form, although a growing number of outlets do take credit cards. Your hard currency can be easily changed at exchange offices, some of which will be located in the stores themselves. Rates offered in stores, however, tend to be worse than in banks and independent foreign exchange offices.

USEFUL WORDS AND PHRASES

airmail	авиапочта	*avee-yapochta*
bank	банк	*bank*
banknote	банкнота	*banknota*
change (*verb*)	обменять	*abmyenyat'*
check	чек	*chyek*
collection	выемка	*vi-yemka*
counter	стойка	*stoyka*
customs form	таможенная	*tamozhena-ya*
	декларация	*dyeklaratsee-ya*
delivery	поставка	*pastafka*
dollar	доллар	*dolar*
exchange rate	обменный курс	*abmyeni koors*
form	бланк	*blank*
international	поручение на	*poruchyeneeye na*
money order	международный	*myezhdoo-narodni*
	перевод	*pyeryevot*
letter	письмо	*pees'mo*
mail	почта	*pochta*
mailbox	почтовый ящик	*pachtovi yasheek*
mailman	почтальон	*pachtal'on*
package	посылка	*pasilka*
postage rates	почтовые тарифы	*pachtoviye tareefi*
postal code	почтовый индекс	*pachtovi eendyeks*
postcard	открытка	*atkritka*
poste-restante	почта до	*pochta da-*
	востребования	*vastryebavanee-ya*
post office	почта	*pochta*
registered letter	заказное письмо	*zakazno-ye pees'mo*
stamp	марка	*marka*
telegram	телеграмма	*tyelyegrama*
traveler's check	дорожный чек	*darozhni chyek*
ZIP code	почтовый индекс	*pachtovi eendyeks*

How much is a postcard to …?
Сколько стоит открытка в …?
skol'ka sto-eet atkritka v …?

I want to register this letter
Я хочу отправить заказное письмо
ya khachoo atpraveet' zakazno-ye pees'mo

I want to send this letter to …
Я хочу отправить это письмо в …
ya khachoo atpraveet' eta pees'mo v …

By airmail, please
Авиапочтой, пожалуйста
avee-apochtay, pazhalsta

How long does the mail to … take?
Сколько это будет идти до …?
skol'ka eta boodyet eetee do …?

Where can I mail this?
Где я могу это отправить?
gdye ya magoo eta atpraveet'?

Is there any mail for me?
Есть письма для меня?
yest' pees'ma dlya myenya?

My last name is …
Моя фамилия …
ma-ya fameelee-ya …

I'd like to send a telegram
Я хочу отправить телеграмму
ya khachoo atpraveet' tyelyegramoo

I'd like to change this into …
Я хочу разменять это на ...
ya khach<u>oo</u> razmyeny<u>at</u>'<u>e</u>ta na …

Can I cash these traveler's checks?
Можно обменять эти дорожные чеки?
m<u>o</u>zhna abmyeny<u>at</u>' <u>e</u>tee dar<u>o</u>zhniye ch<u>ye</u>kee?

What is the exchange rate for the dollar?
Какой курс обмена фунтов долларов?
kak<u>o</u>y koors abm<u>ye</u>na f<u>oo</u>ntaf d<u>o</u>laraf?

THINGS YOU'LL SEE

авиапочта	*avee-yap<u>o</u>chta*	airmail
адрес	*<u>a</u>dryes*	address
адресат	*adryes<u>a</u>t*	addressee
банк	*bank*	bank
денежные переводы	*dyenyezhniye pyeryev<u>o</u>di*	money orders
заказные письма	*zakazniye p<u>ees</u>'ma*	registered mail
заполнить	*zap<u>o</u>lneet'*	fill in
касса	*k<u>a</u>sa*	cash register
марка	*m<u>a</u>rka*	stamp
марки	*m<u>a</u>rkee*	stamps
обмен валюты	*abm<u>ye</u>n valy<u>oo</u>ti*	currency exchange
открытка	*atkr<u>i</u>tka*	postcard
отправитель	*atprav<u>ee</u>tyel'*	sender
пакет	*pak<u>ye</u>t*	package
письмо	*pees'm<u>o</u>*	letter
почта	*p<u>o</u>chta*	mailbox; post office
почта до востребования	*p<u>o</u>chta da vastr<u>ye</u>bavanee-ya*	poste-restante

почтовый индекс	*pachtovi eendyeks*	postal code; ZIP code
приём посылок	*pree-yom pasilak*	package counter
стоимость международной отправки	*sto-eemast' myezhdoonarodnay atpravkee*	postage abroad
тариф	*tareef*	charge
телеграммы	*tyelyegrami*	telegrams
часы работы	*chasi raboti*	opening hours

TELEPHONES

The majority of hotels in the big cities now have international phone booths or satellite phone facilities, so you should be able to make both international and local calls from yours. Hotel phone booths take phonecards (which can normally be bought in the lobby) as well as several major credit cards. If you do not have access to an international direct-dial phone, then your call must be arranged through the operator.

To avoid delay, international calls should be arranged well in advance. Although essential phrases are included below, the operators connecting you will usually speak English. If unable to call from a hotel, you can go to a telephone and telegraph office and make the call from there as a last option.

USEFUL WORDS AND PHRASES

ambulance	скорая помощь (03)	*skora-ya pomash'*
call	звонок	*zvanok*
call (*verb*)	звонить	*zvaneet'*
code	код	*kod*
dial (*verb*)	набирать номер	*nabeerat' nomyer*
dial tone	гудок	*goodok*
extension (*number*)	добавочный (номер)	*dabavachni (nomyer)*
fire	пожар (01)	*pazhar*
inquiries	справочная (09)	*spravachna-ya*
international call	международный звонок	*myezhdoo-narodni zvanok*
number	номер	*nomyer*
pay phone	телефон-автомат	*tyelyefon-aftamat*
police	милиция (02)	*meeleetsee-ya*
receiver	(телефонная) трубка	*(tyelyefona-ya) troopka*
telephone	телефон	*tyelyefon*

telephone booth	телефон-автомат	*tyelyefon-aftamat*
telephone directory	телефонный справочник	*tyelyefoni spravachneek*
wrong number	неправильный номер	*nyepraveel'ni nomyer*

Where is the nearest phone booth?
Где ближайший телефон-автомат?
gdye bleezhIshee tyelyefon-aftamat?

Is there a telephone directory?
У вас есть телефонный справочник?
oo vas yest' tyelyefoni spravachneek?

I would like the directory for …
Мне нужен телефонный справочник для ...
mnye noozhen tyelyefoni spravachneek dlya …

I would like to arrange a call to New York for 8:00 tomorrow evening
Я хочу заказать разговор с Нью-Йорком на восемь вечера завтра
ya khachoo zakazat' razgavor snyuyorkom na vosyem' vyechyera zaftra

Can I call abroad from here?
Можно позвонить за границу отсюда?
mozhna pazvaneet' zagraneetsoo atsyooda?

How much is a call to …?
Сколько стоит звонок в ...?
skol'ka stoeet zvanok v …?

I would like a number in …
Мне нужен номер в …
mnye noozhen nomyer v …

Hello, this is … speaking
Алло, говорит …
allo, gavareet …

Is that …?
Это …?
eta …?

Speaking (*literally: I'm listening*)
Слушаю
sloosha-yoo

I would like to speak to …
Позовите, пожалуйста …
pazaveet-ye pazhalsta …

Extension …, please
Добавочный …, пожалуйста
dabavachni …, pazhalsta

Please say that he/she called
Пожалуйста, передайте, что звонил (*m*)/звонила (*f*)
pazhalsta pyeryedIt-ye shto zvaneel/zvaneela

Ask him/her to call me back, please
Попросите его/её позвонить мне, пожалуйста
papraseet-ye yevo/yeyo pazvaneet' mnye pazhalsta

My number is …
Мой номер …
moy nomyer …

Do you know where he/she is?
Вы знаете, где он/она?
vi znayet-ye gdye on/ana?

When will he/she be back?
Когда он/она вернётся?
kagda on/ana vyernyotsa?

Could you leave him/her a message?
Вы можете передать ему/ей?
vi mozhet-ye pyeryedat' yemoo/yay?

I'll call back later
Я позвоню позже
ya pazvanyoo pozhe

Sorry, wrong number
Вы не туда попали
vi nye tooda papalee

THINGS YOU'LL SEE

автоматический набор	*avtomateechyeskeey nabor*	direct dial
код	*kot*	code
междугородный звонок	*myezhdoo-garodnee zvanok*	long-distance call
международный звонок	*myezhdoo-narodni zvanok*	international call
местный звонок	*myestni zvanok*	local call
милиция	*meeleetsee-ya*	police

→

не работает	*nye rabota-yet*	out of order
пожар	*pazhar*	fire
скорая помощь	*skora-ya pomash'*	ambulance
справочная	*spravachna-ya*	inquiries
стоимость	*sto-eemast'*	charges
телефон	*tyelyefon*	telephone
телефон-автомат	*tyelyefon-aftamat*	telephone booth; pay phone

THINGS YOU'LL HEAR

skyem vi khateet-ye gavareet'?
Who would you like to speak to?

vi nye tooda papalee
You've got the wrong number

kto gavareet?
Who's speaking?

allo
Hello

kakoy oo vas nomyer?
What is your number?

eezveeneet-ye yevo/yeyo nyet
Sorry, he/she's not in

on/ana vernyotsa v …
He/she'll be back at … o'clock

pyeryezvaneet-ye pazhalsta zaftra
Please call again tomorrow

ya pyeryedam shto vi zvaneelee
I'll say that you called

HEALTH

If you become seriously ill during your visit to Russia, notify
the hotel management and Intourist that you need both
medical attention and an interpreter. Sometimes the Russian
doctor treating you will have a good command of English
but, wherever possible, it is worth making arrangements for
an interpreter immediately. This will insure mutual
comprehension between you and your doctor without wasting
any time.

All travelers to Russia should make sure they have adequate
medical insurance, since the quality of local healthcare is not
high and fees for private services can be very expensive.
Travelers feeling the onset of a serious illness may prefer to
return home immediately, if possible. Private companies that
deal with foreigners can arrange medical evacuation via
Finland. If you or someone under your care needs to fly home
urgently, it is always worth checking that all requirements have
been fulfilled for making insurance claims at a later date
(e.g., obtaining doctor's certificates, with details of names,
dates, illnesses, etc.).

In less urgent cases of illness, you should, with the help of
the phrases and vocabulary below, be able to fend for yourself.

USEFUL WORDS AND PHRASES

accident	несчастный случай	*nyesh<u>a</u>stni sl<u>oo</u>chI*
ambulance	скорая помощь	*sk<u>o</u>ra-ya p<u>o</u>mash'*
appendicitis	аппендицит	*apyendeets<u>ee</u>t*
appendix	аппендикс	*apy<u>e</u>ndeeks*
aspirin	аспирин	*aspeer<u>ee</u>n*
asthma	астма	*<u>a</u>stma*
backache	боль в спине	*bol' vspeen<u>ye</u>*
bandage	бинт	*beent*
(adhesive)	пластырь	*pl<u>a</u>stir'*

bite *(by dog)*	укус (собаки)	*ook<u>oo</u>s (sab<u>a</u>kee)*
(by insect)	укус (насекомого)	*ook<u>oo</u>s (nasyek<u>o</u>mava)*
bladder	мочевой пузырь	*machyev<u>o</u>y poozir'*
blister	волдырь	*vald<u>i</u>r'*
blood	кровь	*krof'*
burn *(noun)*	ожог	*azh<u>o</u>k*
cancer	рак	*rak*
chest	грудь	*groot'*
chicken pox	ветрянка	*vyetr<u>ya</u>nka*
cold *(noun)*	простуда	*prast<u>oo</u>da*
concussion	контузия	*kant<u>oo</u>zee-ya*
constipation	запор	*zap<u>o</u>r*
contact lenses	контактные линзы	*kant<u>a</u>ktniye l<u>ee</u>nzi*
corn	мозоль	*maz<u>o</u>l'*
cough *(noun)*	кашель	*k<u>a</u>shel'*
cut	порез	*par<u>ye</u>s*
dentist	зубной врач	*zoobn<u>o</u>y vrach*
diabetes	диабет	*dee-ab<u>ye</u>t*
diarrhea	понос	*pan<u>o</u>s*
dizziness	головокружение	*galava-kroozh<u>e</u>neeye*
doctor *(profession)*	врач	*vrach*
doctor *(as form of address)*	доктор	*d<u>o</u>ktar*
drugstore	аптека	*apt<u>ye</u>ka*
earache	боль в ухе	*bol' v<u>oo</u>kh-ye*
fever	температура	*tyempyerat<u>oo</u>ra*
filling	пломба	*pl<u>o</u>mba*
first aid	первая помощь	*p<u>ye</u>rva-ya p<u>o</u>mash'*
flu	грипп	*greep*
fracture	перелом	*pyeryel<u>o</u>m*
German measles	краснуха	*krasn<u>oo</u>kha*
glasses	очки	*achk<u>ee</u>*
gum	десна	*dyesn<u>a</u>*

hayfever	сенная лихорадка	*syennaya leekharadka*
headache	головная боль	*galavna-ya bol'*
heart	сердце	*syertse*
heart attack	сердечный приступ	*syerdyechni preestoop*
hemorrhage	кровотечение	*kravatyechyeneeye*
hospital	больница	*bal'-neetsa*
ill	болен (m)	*bolyen*
	больна (f)	*bal'na*
indigestion	несварение	*nyesvaryeneeye*
infected	заражённый	*zarazhyoni*
injection	укол	*ookol*
itch	зуд	*zoot*
kidney	почка	*pochka*
lump	опухоль	*opookhal'*
measles	корь	*kor'*
migraine	мигрень	*meegryen'*
mumps	свинка	*sveenka*
nausea	тошнота	*tashnata*
nurse	медсестра	*myedsyestra*
operation	операция	*apyeratsee-ya*
optician	окулист	*akooleest*
pain	боль	*bol'*
penicillin	пенициллин	*pyeneetseeleen*
plaster (*of Paris*)	гипс	*geeps*
pneumonia	пневмония	*pnyevmanee-ya*
pregnant	беременная	*byeryemyena-ya*
prescription	рецепт	*ryetsyept*
rheumatism	ревматизм	*ryevmateezm*
scratch	царапина	*tsarapeena*
sore throat	боль в горле	*bol' vgorl-ye*
splinter	заноза	*zanoza*
sprain	растяжение связок	*rastyazheneeye svyazak*

sting	укус	*ookoos*
stomach	желудок	*zheloodak*
temperature	температура	*tyempyeratoora*
tonsils	миндалины	*meendaleeni*
toothache	зубная боль	*zoobna-ya bol'*
ulcer	язва	*yazva*
vaccination	прививка	*preeveefk*
whooping cough	коклюш	*kaklyoosh*

I feel sick
Меня тошнит
myenya tashneet

I have motion sickness
Меня укачало
myenya ookachala

I have a pain in ...
У меня болит ...
oo myenya baleet ...

I do not feel well
Мне плохо
mnye plokha

I feel faint
Мне дурно
mnye doorna

I feel dizzy
У меня кружится голова
oo myenya kroozheetsa galava

It hurts here
Болит здесь
baleet zdyes'

It's a sharp pain
Острая боль
ostra-ya bol'

It's a dull pain
Тупая боль
toopa-ya bol'

It hurts all the time
Болит всё время
baleet vsyo vryemya

It only hurts now and then
Болит время от времени
baleet vryema at vryemyenee

It hurts when you touch it
Болит, когда вы трогаете
baleet kagda vi troga-yet-ye

It hurts more at night
Болит сильнее ночью
baleet seel'nyeye nochyoo

It stings
Жжёт
zhyot

It aches
Болит
baleet

I have a temperature
У меня температура
oo myenya tyempyeratoora

I need a prescription for ...
Мне нужен рецепт для ...
mnye noozhen ryetsyept dlya ...

I normally take ...
Обычно я принимаю ...
abichna ya preeneema-yoo ...

I'm allergic to ...
У меня аллергия на ...
oo myenya allyergee-ya na ...

Have you got anything for ...?
У вас есть что-нибудь от ...?
oo vas yest' shto-neeboot' ot ...?

Do I need a prescription for this?
Мне нужен рецепт для этого?
mnye noozhen ryetsyept dlya etava?

I have lost a filling
У меня выпала пломба
oo myenya vipala plomba

THINGS YOU'LL SEE

больница	*bal'neetsa*	hospital
врач	*vrach*	doctor
дежурная аптека	*dyezhoorna-ya aptyeka*	pharmacist on duty
зубной врач	*zoobnoy vrach*	dentist
клиника	*kleeneeka*	clinic
кровяное давление	*kravyano-ye davlyeneeye*	blood pressure
лекарство	*lyekarstva*	medicine
нарыв	*nariv*	abscess
натощак	*natashak*	on an empty stomach
окулист	*akooleest*	optician
осмотр	*asmotr*	checkup
отолоринголог	*atalareengolak*	ear, nose, and throat specialist
очки	*achkee*	glasses
пломба	*plomba*	filling
поликлиника	*paleekleeneeka*	surgery
пункт скорой помощи	*poonkt skoray pomashee*	First Aid Center
рентген	*ryentgyen*	X-ray
рецепт	*ryetsyept*	prescription
скорая помощь	*skora-ya pomash'*	ambulance
укол	*ookol*	injection

THINGS YOU'LL HEAR

preeneem<u>I</u>t-ye po ... tabl<u>ye</u>tkee
Take ... tablets at a time

svad<u>oy</u>
With water

razzh<u>oo</u>yt-ye
Chew them

ad<u>ee</u>n raz/dva r<u>a</u>za/tree r<u>a</u>za vdyen'
Once/twice/three times a day

tol'ka py<u>e</u>ryed snom
Only when you go to bed

shto vi ab<u>i</u>chna preeneem<u>a</u>-yet-ye?
What do you normally take?

vam n<u>oo</u>zhna pI<u>tee</u> kvrach<u>oo</u>
I think you should see a doctor

eezveen<u>ee</u>t-ye oo nas <u>e</u>tava nyet
I'm sorry, we don't have that

dlya <u>e</u>tava vam n<u>oo</u>zhen ryetsy<u>e</u>pt
For that you need a prescription

MINI-DICTIONARY

about: about 16 okala shesnatsatee
absorbent cotton vata
accident avaree-ya
accommodations razmyeshyeneeye
ache bol'
adaptor transfarmatar
address adryes
after posl-ye
aftershave adyekalon
again snova
against proteef
air conditioning kandeetsee-anyer
aircraft samalyot
airline avee-aleenee-ya
airport aeraport
alarm clock boodeel'neek
alcohol alkagol'
all vyes'
  all the streets fsye ooleetsi
  that's all, thanks fsyo, spaseeba
almost pachtee
alone adeen
already oozhe
always fsyegda
ambulance skora-ya pomash'
America amyereeka
American amyereekanskee
  (male) amyereekanyets
  (female) amyereekanka
and ee
ankle ladishka
anorak koortka
another: another room droogoy
  nomyer
  another coffee yeshyo kof-ye
antifreeze anteefreez
antiques shop anteekvarni magazeen
apartment kvarteera

aperitif apyereeteef
appetite apyeteet
apple yablaka
application form blank
appointment zapees'
apricot abreekos
arm rooka
art eeskoostva
art gallery khoodozhestvena-ya
  galyerya-ya
artist khoodozhneek
as: as soon as possible kak mozhna
  skarye-ye
ashtray pyepyel'neetsa
aspirin aspeereen
at: at the post office na pocht-ye
  at night noch'yoo
  at 3:00 ftree chasa
attractive preevlyekatyel'ni
aunt tyotya
Australia afstralee-ya
Australian afstraleeskee
  (male) afstraleeyets
  (female) afstraleeka
auto-body shop stantsee-ya
  tyekh-absloozheevanee-ya
automatic afta-mateechyeskee
away: is it far away? eta dalyeko?
  go away! ookhadeet-ye!
awful oozhasni
ax tapor

baby ryebyonak
baby carriage dyetska-ya kalyaska
back (not front) nazat
  (body) speena
backpack ryookzak

bad plakh<u>oy</u>

baggage bag<u>a</u>sh

baggage rack bag<u>a</u>zhna-ya p<u>o</u>lka

baggage locker k<u>a</u>myera khran<u>ye</u>nee-ya

bakery b<u>oo</u>lachna-ya

balalaika balal<u>l</u>ka

balcony balk<u>o</u>n

ball myach

ballet bal<u>ye</u>t

ballpoint pen sh<u>a</u>reekava-ya r<u>oo</u>chka

Baltic (states) preeb<u>a</u>lteeka

banana ban<u>a</u>n

band (musicians) ark<u>ye</u>str

bandage beent

    (adhesive) pl<u>a</u>stir'

bank bank

banknote bankn<u>o</u>ta

bar bar

    bar of chocolate pl<u>ee</u>tka shakal<u>a</u>da

barbershop pareekhm<u>a</u>khyerska-ya

basement padv<u>a</u>l

basket karz<u>ee</u>na

bath v<u>a</u>na

    to have a bath preeneem<u>a</u>t' v<u>a</u>noo

bathing cap koop<u>a</u>l'na-ya sh<u>a</u>pachka

bathing suit koop<u>a</u>l'ni kast<u>yoo</u>m

bathroom v<u>a</u>na-ya

battery batar<u>ya</u>yka

beach plyash

beans fas<u>o</u>l'

beard barad<u>a</u>

because patam<u>oo</u> shto

bed krav<u>a</u>t'

bed linen past<u>ye</u>l'na-ye byel'<u>yo</u>

bedroom sp<u>a</u>l'nya

beef gav<u>ya</u>deena

beer p<u>ee</u>va

before do

beginner nacheen<u>a</u>-yooshee

behind za

beige b<u>ye</u>zhevi

bell (church) k<u>o</u>lakal

    (door) zvan<u>o</u>k

Belorussia byelar<u>oo</u>see-ya

below pod

belt p<u>o</u>-yas

beside <u>o</u>kala

best l<u>oo</u>chee

better l<u>oo</u>che

between my<u>e</u>zhdoo

bicycle vyelaseep<u>ye</u>d

big bal'sh<u>oy</u>

bikini koop<u>a</u>l'neek

bill shyot

bird pt<u>ee</u>tsa

birthday dyen' razhd<u>ye</u>nee-ya

    happy birthday! zdnyom
    razhd<u>ye</u>nee-ya!

bite (verb) koos<u>a</u>t'

    (noun) ook<u>oo</u>s

    (by insect) nasyek<u>o</u>mava

bitter g<u>o</u>r'kee

black ch<u>yo</u>rni

black currant ch<u>yo</u>rna-ya smar<u>o</u>deena

Black Sea ch<u>yo</u>rna-ye m<u>o</u>r-ye

blanket ady<u>e</u>yala

bleach (verb: hair) v<u>i</u>svyetleet'

blind (cannot see) slyep<u>oy</u>

blister vald<u>i</u>r

blood krof'

blouse bl<u>oo</u>ska

blue s<u>ee</u>nee

boat parakh<u>o</u>t

    (smaller) l<u>o</u>tka

body t<u>ye</u>la

bolt (on door) bolt

bone kost'

book kn<u>ee</u>ga

bookstore kn<u>ee</u>zhni magaz<u>ee</u>n

boot sap<u>o</u>g

    (rubber) ryez<u>ee</u>naviye sapag<u>ee</u>

border gran<u>ee</u>tsa

boring sk<u>oo</u>shni

born: I was born in …

    (male) ya rad<u>ee</u>lsa v …

    (female) ya rad<u>ee</u>las' v …

both oba
  both of them anee oba
  both of us mi oba
  both ... and ... ee ... ee ...
bottle bootilka
bottle opener shtopar
bottle cap propka
bottom dno
bowl chashka
box karopka
boy mal'cheek
boyfriend drook
bra byoostgal'tyer
bracelet braslyet
brandy kan'yak
bread khlyep
break (noun) pyeryerif
  (verb) lamat'
breakdown (car) palomka
  (nervous) nyervna-ye rastroystva
breakfast zaftrak
breathe dishat'
  I can't breathe mnye troodna dishat'
bridge most
briefcase partfyel'
British breetanskee
brochure brashyoora
broil greel'
broken slomani
  broken leg slomana-ya naga
brooch brosh
brother brat
brown kareechnyevi
bruise seenyak
brush (noun) shyotka
  (paint) keest'
bucket vyedro
bug (in room) klop
building zdaneeye
Bulgarian balgarskee
burglar vor
burn (verb) abzheegat'
  (noun) azhok

bus aftoboos
  bus station aftoboosna-ya
  stantsee-ya
business dyela
  it's none of your business
  eta nye vashe dyela
busy (occupied) zanyat
but no
butcher myasnoy magazeen
butter masla
button poogavyetsa
buy pakoopat'
by: by the window okala akna

cabbage kapoosta
café kafe
cake kyeks
calculator kal'koolyatar
call (summon) zvat'
  (telephone) zvaneet'
  what's it called? kak eta naziva-yetsa?
camera fata-aparat
camper (trailer) dom-aftafoorgon
campsite kyempeeng
can (vessel) banka
  can opener kansyervni nosh
  can I have ...? mozhna ...?
Canada kanada
Canadian kanatskee
  (male) kanadyets
  (female) kanatka
cancer rak
candle svyecha
candy kanfyetka
canoe kanoe
cap (hat) kyepka
car masheena
carbonated sheepoochee
card atkritka
cardigan kofta
careful astarozhni
  be careful! astarozhna!
carpet kavyor

carriage *(train)* vag<u>o</u>n
carrot mark<u>of</u>'
case chyemad<u>a</u>n
cash nal<u>ee</u>chniye
  (coins) man<u>ye</u>ti
  to pay cash plat<u>ee</u>t' nal<u>ee</u>chnimee
Caspian Sea kasp<u>ee</u>skaye m<u>o</u>r-ye
cassette kas<u>ye</u>ta
cassette player magneetaf<u>o</u>n
castle z<u>a</u>mak
cat k<u>o</u>shka
cathedral sab<u>o</u>r
Caucasus kafk<u>a</u>s
cauliflower tsvyetn<u>a</u>-ya kap<u>oo</u>sta
cave pyeshy<u>e</u>ra
cemetery kl<u>a</u>dbeesh-ye
center tsy<u>e</u>ntr
certificate oodastavyer<u>ye</u>neeye
chair stool
chambermaid g<u>o</u>rneechna-ya
change *(noun: money)* abm<u>ye</u>n
  (verb: clothes) pyerye-adyev<u>a</u>t'sa
  (verb: money) razmyen<u>ya</u>t'
cheers! *(toast)* v<u>a</u>she zdar<u>o</u>v'ye!
cheese sir
check chyek
checkbook chy<u>e</u>kava-ya kn<u>ee</u>zhka
cherry v<u>ee</u>shnya
chess sh<u>a</u>khmati
chest groot'
chewing gum zhev<u>a</u>tyel'na-ya
  ryez<u>ee</u>nka
chicken k<u>oo</u>reetsa
child ryeby<u>o</u>nak
children d<u>ye</u>tee
China keet<u>I</u>
chocolate shakal<u>a</u>t
  box of chocolates kar<u>o</u>pka
  shakal<u>a</u>dnikh kanf<u>ye</u>t
chop *(food)* atbeevn<u>a</u>-ya
  (cut) roob<u>ee</u>t'
church ts<u>e</u>rkaf'
cigar seeg<u>a</u>ra

cigarette seegar<u>ye</u>ta
circus tseerk
city g<u>o</u>rat
city center tsyentr g<u>o</u>rada
class klas
classical music klas<u>ee</u>chyeska-ya
  m<u>oo</u>zika
clean ch<u>ee</u>sti
clear *(obvious)* y<u>a</u>sni
  is that clear? <u>e</u>ta y<u>a</u>sna?
clever <u>oo</u>mni
clock chas<u>i</u>
close *(near)* bl<u>ee</u>skee
  (stuffy) d<u>oo</u>shni
  (verb) zakriv<u>a</u>t'
  the store is closed magaz<u>ee</u>n zakr<u>i</u>t
clothes ady<u>e</u>zhda
club kloop
coat pal't<u>o</u>
coathanger vy<u>e</u>shalka
cockroach tarak<u>a</u>n
coffee k<u>o</u>f-ye
coin man<u>ye</u>ta
cold *(illness)* greep
  (adj.) khal<u>o</u>dni
collar varatn<u>ee</u>k
collection *(stamps, etc.)*
  kal<u>ye</u>ktsee-ya
collective *(noun)* kalyekt<u>ee</u>f
color tsvyet
color film tsvyetn<u>a</u>-ya ply<u>o</u>nka
comb *(noun)* raschy<u>o</u>ska
  (verb) preechy<u>o</u>sivat'sa
come preekhad<u>ee</u>t'
  I come from … ya eez …
  come here! eed<u>ee</u>t-ye sy<u>oo</u>da!
Communist Party
  kamoonest<u>ee</u>chyeska-ya p<u>a</u>rtee-ya
compartment k<u>oo</u>pe
complicated sl<u>o</u>zhni
concert kants<u>ye</u>rt
conductor *(bus)* kand<u>oo</u>ktar
  (orchestra) deereezhy<u>o</u>r

congratulations! pazdravlya-yoo!

constipation zapor

consulate konsoolstva

contact lenses kantaktniye leenzi

contraceptive
prateeva-zachatachna-ye sryedstva

cook (noun) povar
(verb) gatoveet'

cookie pyechyen'ye

cooking utensils kookhaniye
preenadlyezhnastee

cool prakhladni

cork propka

corkscrew shtopar

corner oogal

corridor kareedor

cosmetics kasmyeteeka

Cossack kazak

cost (verb) sto-eet'
what does it cost? skol'ka
eta sto-eet?

cotton khlopak

cotton balls vata

cough (verb) kashlyat'
(noun) kashel'

cough drops tablyetkee at kashlya

country (state) strana
(not town) dyeryevnya

course: of course kanyeshna

cousin (male) dvayooradni brat
(female) dvayooradna-ya syestra

crab krap

cream sleefkee

credit card kryedeetna-ya kartachka

crew ekeepash

Crimea krim

crowded pyeryepolnyeni

cruise kroo-ees

crutches kastilee

cry (weep) plakat'
(shout) kreechat'

cucumber agooryets

cuff links zapankee

cup chashka

cupboard shkaf

curtain zanavyeska

customs tamozhnya

cut (noun) paryez
(verb) ryezat'

dad papa

damp siroy

dance tanyets

dangerous apasni

dark tyomni

date cheeslo

daughter doch'

day dyen'

dead myortvi

deaf glookhoy

dear daragoy

deck chair shezlong

deep gloobokee

delay zadyershka

deliberately narochna

dentist zoobnoy vrach

dentures pratyez

deodorant dyezadarant

depart (verb) oo-yezhat'

department store ooneevyermak

develop (a roll of film) pra-yavlyat'

diamond breelee-ant

diaper pyelyonka

diarrhea panos

diary dnyevneek

dictionary slavar'

die oomeerat'

diesel deezyel

diet dee-yeta

different (other) droogoy
(various) razni
that's different eta droogo-ye dyela

difficult troodni

dining room stalova-ya

dinner abyet

directory *(telephone)* tyelyef**o**ni
spr**a**vachneek
dirty gry**a**zni
disabled eenval**e**et
dishwashing liquid zh**e**edkast' dlya
mit'**ya** pas**oo**di
dive nir**ya**t'
diving board trampl**ee**n
divorced *(male)* razvyed**yo**ni
(female) razvyedyen**a**
do d**ye**lat'
dock preech**a**l
doctor vrach
document dako**o**m**ye**nt
dog sab**a**ka
doll k**oo**kla
dollar d**o**lar
door dvyer'
double room n**o**myer sdvoosp**a**l'nay
krav**a**t'yoo
down fnees
dress pl**a**t'ye
drink *(verb)* peet'
(noun) nap**ee**tak
drinking water peet'yev**a**-ya vad**a**
drive *(verb)* vad**ee**t'
driver vad**ee**tyel'
driver's license vad**ee**tyel'sk**ee**ye prav**a**
drunk p'**ya**ni
dry s**oo**kh**o**y
dry cleaner kh**ee**mch**ee**stka
during va-vr**ye**mya
dust cloth tr**ya**pka dlya p**i**lee
duty-free byesp**o**shleena-ya targ**o**vlya

each *(every)* k**a**zhdi
twenty roubles each dv**a**tsat'
roobl**ya**y k**a**zhdi
ear **oo**kha
(plural) **oo**shee
early r**a**na
earrings s**ye**r'gee

east vast**o**k
Easter p**a**skha
easy l**yo**khkee
eat yest'
egg ylts**o**
elastic ryez**ee**nka
elbow l**o**kat'
electric elyektr**ee**chyeskee
electricity elyektr**ee**chyestva
elevator leeft
else: something else sht**o**-ta yesh**yo**
someone else kt**o**-ta yesh**yo**
somewhere else gdye-ta yesh**yo**
embarrassed smoosh**yo**ni
embassy pas**o**l'stva
emerald eezoomr**oo**t
emergency cord stop-kran
emergency exit zapasn**o**y v**i**khat
empty poost**o**y
end kan**ye**ts
engaged *(couple)* pam**o**lvlyeni
(occupied) z**a**nyat
engine *(motor)* dv**ee**gatyel'
England angl**ee**-ya
English
(language) angl**ee**skee yaz**i**k
Englishman angleech**a**neen
Englishwoman angleech**a**nka
enlargement oovyeleech**ye**neeye
enough dast**a**tachna
enter fkhad**ee**t'
entertainment razvl**ye**ch**ye**neeye
entrance fkhot
envelope kanv**ye**rt
eraser ryez**ee**nka
especially as**o**byena
Europe yevr**o**pa
evening v**ye**chyer
every k**a**zhdi
everyone fsye
everything fsyo
everywhere vyezd-**ye**

example preemyer
  for example napreemyer
excellent atleechni
excess baggage pyeryevyes bagazha
exchange (*verb*) myenyat'
exchange rate valyootni koors
excursion ekskoorsee-ya
excuse me! (*to get past*) eezveeneet-ye!
  (*to get attention*) prasteet-ye!
  (*as a question*) prasteet-ye?
exhibition vistafka
exit vikhat
expensive daragoy
explain abyasnyat'
eye drops glazniye kaplee
eyes glaza

fabric tkan'
face leetso
fact fakt
faint (*unclear*) tooskli
  (*verb*) tyeryat' saznaneeye
fair (*amusement park*) yarmarka
  (*just*) spravyedleevi
fall (*verb*) padat'
false teeth pratyez
family syem'ya
fan (*ventilator*) vyenteelyatar
  (*enthusiast*) balyel'sheek
far dalyeko
fare sto-eemast' prayezda
farm fyerma
farmer fyermyer
fashion moda
fast bistro
fat (*person*) tolsti
  (*on meat, etc.*) zheer
father atyets
feel (*touch*) choostvavat'
  I feel hot mnye zharka
  I don't feel well mnye plokha
feet nogee

felt-tip pen flamastyer
female zhenskee
ferry parom
fever leekharatka
few nyeskal'ka
fiancé zheneekh
fiancée nyevyesta
field pol-ye
fill in zapalnyat'
filling (*tooth*) plomba
fill up napolnyat'
film (*movie*) feel'm
  (*camera*) plyonka
filter feeltr
find (*verb*) nakhadeet'
finger palyets
Finland feenlyandee-ya
fire (*blaze*) pazhar
fire exit pazharni vikhat
fire extinguisher agnyetoosheetyel'
firework salyoot
first pyervi
first aid skora-ya pomash'
first name eemya
fish riba
fishing ribna-ya lovlya
  to go fishing khadeet' na ribalkoo
fishing rod oodachka
fishmonger ribni magazeen
flag flak
flash (*camera*) fspishka
flashlight fanareek
flat ploskee
flavor fkoos
flea blakha
flight ryays
flight attendant
  (*male*) bart-pravadneek
  (*female*) styoo-ardyesa
floor (*of building*) etash
  (*of room*) pol
flour mooka
flower tsvyetok

flu greep
flute flyayta
fly (*verb*) lyetyet'
  (*insect*) mookha
fog tooman
folk music narodna-ya moozika
food yeda
food poisoning peeshevo-ye atravlyeneeye
foot naga
  on foot pyeshkom
for dlya
  for me dlya myenya
  what for? dlya chyevo?
forbid zapryeshat'
foreigner
  (*male*) eenostranyets
  (*female*) eenostranka
forest lyes
fork veelka
fountain pen aftaroochka
fourth chyetvyorti
fracture pyeryelom
free svabodni
  (*no cost*) byesplatni
freezer marazeel'neek
French frantsoozskee
French fries kartofyel' free
friend (*male*) drook
  (*female*) padrooga
friendly droozheskee
from ot
  I'm from Chicago ya eez Cheekago
front: in front of pyeryet
frost maros
frozen (*adj.*) zamyorz
fruit frookt
fruit juice frooktovi sok
fry zhareet'
frying pan skavarada
full polni
  I'm full (*male*) ya sit
  (*female*) ya sita

funny (*amusing*) smyeshnoy
  (*odd*) strani
fur myekh
fur hat myekhava-ya shapka
furniture myebel'

game eegra
garbage moosar
garbage can moosarni yasheek
garden sat
garlic chyesnok
gas byenzeen
gas station byenzakalonka
gay (*homosexual*) galooboy
gear pyeryedacha
Georgia groozee-ya
German nyemyetskee
get (*fetch*) dastavat'
  have you got …? oo vas yest' …?
  to get the train oospyet' na po-yest
get back (*return*) vazvrashat'sa
get in/on (*to vehicle*) sadeet'sa
get out vikhadeet'
get up (*rise*) fstavat'
gift padarak
gin dzheen
girl dyevooshka
girlfriend padrooga
give davat'
glad rat
  I'm glad (*male*) ya rat
  (*female*) ya rada
glasnost glasnast'
glass (*for drinking*) stakan
  (*material*) styeklo
glasses achkee
gloves pyerchatkee
glue klay
goggles zasheetniye achkee
gold zolata
good kharoshee
  good! kharasho

good-bye dasveed<u>a</u>nee-ya
government prav<u>ee</u>tyel'stva
granddaughter fn<u>oo</u>chka
grandfather dyed<u>oo</u>shka
grandmother bab<u>oo</u>shka
grandson fnook
grapes veenagr<u>a</u>t
grass trav<u>a</u>
gray s<u>y</u>eri
Great Britain vyeleekabreet<u>a</u>nee-ya
green zyely<u>o</u>ni
grocery store bak<u>a</u>lyeya
ground floor p<u>y</u>ervi et<u>a</u>sh
guarantee
  (noun) gar<u>a</u>ntee-ya
  (verb) garant<u>ee</u>ravat'
guard st<u>o</u>rash
guest gost'
guide book pootyevad<u>ee</u>tyel'
guitar geet<u>a</u>ra
gun *(rifle)* roozh'<u>yo</u>

hair v<u>o</u>lasi
haircut str<u>ee</u>shka
hairdresser pareekm<u>a</u>khyer
hair dryer fyen
hair spray lak dlya val<u>o</u>s
half palav<u>ee</u>na
  half an hour polchas<u>a</u>
ham vyetch<u>ee</u>na
hammer mal<u>a</u>tok
hand rook<u>a</u>
handbag d<u>a</u>mska-ya s<u>oo</u>mka
handkerchief nasav<u>o</u>y plat<u>o</u>k
handle *(door)* r<u>oo</u>chka
handsome kras<u>ee</u>vi
hangover pakhm<u>y</u>el'ye
happy shasl<u>ee</u>vi
harbor g<u>a</u>van'
hard tv<u>y</u>ordi
  (difficult) tyazh<u>yo</u>li
hat shl<u>y</u>apa

112

have eemy<u>e</u>t'
  I don't have … oo myeny<u>a</u> nyet …
  have you got …? oo vas yest' …?
  I have to go now mnye par<u>a</u>
hayfever syen<u>a</u>-ya leekhar<u>a</u>tka
he on
head gal<u>a</u>va
headache galavn<u>a</u>-ya bol'
health zdar<u>o</u>v'ye
hear sl<u>i</u>shat'
hearing aid sl<u>oo</u>khav<u>oy</u> <u>a</u>pp<u>a</u>r<u>a</u>t
heart s<u>y</u>erts-ye
heart attack syerdy<u>e</u>chni pr<u>ee</u>stoop
heating ataply<u>e</u>neeye
heavy tyazh<u>o</u>li
heel *(foot)* p<u>y</u>atka
  (shoe) kabl<u>oo</u>k
hello zdr<u>a</u>stvooyt-ye
help *(noun)* p<u>o</u>mash'
  (verb) pamag<u>a</u>t'
  help! pamag<u>ee</u>t-ye!
her: for her dlya ny<u>e</u>yo
  give it to her atd<u>i</u>t-ye yay
  her bag/bags y<u>e</u>yo s<u>oo</u>mka/s<u>oo</u>mkee
  her house y<u>e</u>yo dom
  her shoes y<u>e</u>yo t<u>oo</u>flee
  it's hers <u>e</u>ta y<u>e</u>yo
high vis<u>o</u>kee
highway afta-str<u>a</u>da
hill kholm
him: for him dlya nyev<u>o</u>
  give it to him atd<u>i</u>t-ye yem<u>oo</u>
hire prak<u>a</u>t
his: his book/books yev<u>o</u>
  kn<u>ee</u>ga/kn<u>ee</u>gee
  his house yev<u>o</u> dom
  it's his <u>e</u>ta yev<u>o</u>
history eest<u>o</u>ree-ya
hitchhike pootyesh<u>e</u>stvavat' afta-st<u>o</u>pam
hobby kh<u>o</u>bee
holiday <u>o</u>tpoosk
home dom
  at home d<u>o</u>ma

honest ch<u>ye</u>sni
honey my<u>o</u>t
honeymoon myed<u>o</u>vi m<u>ye</u>syats
hood (car) kap<u>o</u>t
hope (verb) nad<u>ye</u>yat'sa
  (noun) nad<u>ye</u>zhda
horn (car) s<u>ee</u>gnal
  (animal) rok
horrible ooz<u>ha</u>sni
horse l<u>o</u>shat'
hospital bal'n<u>ee</u>tsa
hot water bottle gr<u>ye</u>lka
hour chas
house dom
how? kak?
  how much? sk<u>o</u>l'ka?
Hungary v<u>ye</u>ngree-ya
hungry: I'm hungry (male) ya gal<u>o</u>dyen
  (female) ya gal<u>o</u>dna
hurry: I'm in a hurry ya spyesh<u>oo</u>
hurt (verb) bal<u>ye</u>t'
husband moosh

I ya
ice lyot
ice cream mar<u>o</u>zhena-ye
ice hockey khaky<u>ay</u>
ice skates kan'k<u>ee</u>
ice skating kat<u>a</u>t'sa na kan'k<u>a</u>kh
icicle sas<u>oo</u>l'ka
icon eek<u>o</u>na
if y<u>e</u>slee
ill (male) bal'n<u>oy</u>
  (female) bal'n<u>a</u>-ya
illness bal<u>ye</u>zn'
immediately nyemy<u>e</u>dlena
important v<u>a</u>zhni
impossible nyevazm<u>o</u>zhna
in v
  in English pa-angl<u>ee</u>skee
  in the hotel v gast<u>ee</u>neets-ye
Indian eend<u>ee</u>skee

indigestion nyesvar<u>ye</u>neeye
  zhel<u>oo</u>tka
inexpensive dyeshy<u>o</u>vi
infection eenf<u>ye</u>ktsee-ya
information eenfarm<u>a</u>tsee-ya
information office spr<u>a</u>vachna-ye
  byoor<u>o</u>
injection een<u>ye</u>ktsee-ya
injury r<u>a</u>na
ink chyern<u>ee</u>la
insect nasyek<u>o</u>ma-ye
insect repellent sr<u>ye</u>dstva ot
  nasyek<u>o</u>mikh
insomnia byes<u>o</u>neetsa
insurance strakh<u>o</u>fka
interesting eentyery<u>e</u>sni
international myezhdoo-nar<u>o</u>dni
interpret pyereyevad<u>ee</u>t'
interpreter pyereyev<u>o</u>tcheek
into v
invitation preeglash<u>e</u>neeye
Ireland eerl<u>a</u>ndee-ya
Irish eerl<u>a</u>ntskee
Irishman eerl<u>a</u>ndyets
Irishwoman eerl<u>a</u>ndka
iron (metal) zhel<u>ye</u>za
  (for clothes) oot<u>yoo</u>k
Iron Curtain zhel<u>ye</u>zni z<u>a</u>navyes
island <u>o</u>straf
it <u>e</u>ta
itch (noun) chyes<u>o</u>tka
  it itches chy<u>e</u>shetsa

jacket peedzh<u>a</u>k
jam var<u>ye</u>n'ye
jazz dzhas
jealous ryevn<u>ee</u>vi
jeans dzh<u>ee</u>nsi
jellyfish myed<u>oo</u>za
jeweler yoovyel<u>ee</u>r
job rab<u>o</u>ta
jog (verb) b<u>ye</u>gat' troosts<u>oy</u>

jogging suit tryeneerovachni
  kastyoom
joke shootka
journey payestka
jump (*verb*) prigat'
just tol'ka/tol'ka shto

key klyooch
KGB ka-ge-be
kidney pochka
kilo keelo
kilometer keelamyetr
kind dobri
kitchen kookhnya
knee kalyena
knife nosh
knit vyazat'
know: I don't know ya nye zna-yoo
Kremlin kryeml'

label eteekyetka
lace kroozheva
laces (*of shoe*) shnoorkee
lake ozyera
lamb (*meat*) baraneena
lamp lampa
lampshade abazhoor
land (*noun*) zyemlya
  (*verb*) preezyemlyat'sa
language yazik
large bal'shoy
last (*final*) paslyednee
  last week na proshlay nyedyel-ye
  last month fproshlam myesyats-ye
  at last! nakanyets
late: it's getting late pozna
  the bus is late aftoboos
  apazdiva-yet
laugh smyeyat'sa
laundromat prachyechna-ya
  sama-absloozheevaneeye

laundry (*place*) prachyechna-ya
  (*dirty clothes*) gryazna-ye byel'yo
laundry detergent steeral'ni parashok
laxative slabeetyel'na-ye
lazy lyeneevi
leaf leest
leaflet leestofka
learn (*language*) eezoochat'
leather kozha
leave (*something somewhere*)
  astavlyat'
  (*in vehicle*) oo-yez-zhat'
  (*on foot*) ookhadeet'
left (*not right*) lyevi
  there's nothing left neechyevo
  nye astalas'
leg naga
lemon leemon
lemonade leemanat
length dleena
Leningrad lyeneengrat
Lenin Library beeblee-atyeka
  eemyenee lyeneena
Lenin's Mausoleum mavzalyay
  lyeneena
lens leenza
less myen'she
lesson oorok
letter pees'mo
lettuce salat-latook
library beeblee-atyeka
license vadeetyel'skeeye prava
life zheezn'
light (*not heavy*) lyokhkee
  (*not dark*) svyetli
lighter zazheegalka
lighter fuel byenzeen dlya zazheegalkee
like: I like you ti mnye nraveesh'sa
  I like swimming mnye nraveetsa
  plavat'
  it's like … eta kak …
line (*of people*) ochyeryet'
  stand in line stayat'vochyeryedee

lip gooba

lipstick goobna-ya pamada

liqueur leekyor

list speesak

listen slooshat'

liter leetr

Lithuania leetva

little (small) malyen'kee

a little nyemnoga

liver pyechyen'

lollipop lyedyenyets

long dleeni

look at smatryet'

look for eeskat'

lose tyeryat'

lost and found office byooro nakhodak

lot: a lot mnoga

loud gromkee

lounge gasteena-ya

love (noun) lyoobof'

(verb) lyoobeet'

low neezkee

luck oodacha

good luck! zhela-yoo oodachee!

lunch abyet

magazine zhoornal

mail (noun) pochta

(verb) pasilat'

mailbox pachtovi yasheek

mailman pachtal'on

make dyelat'

makeup greem

male moozhskoy

man moozhcheena

manager admeeneestrator

many mnoga

map karta

a map of Moscow karta maskvi

marble mramar

margarine margareen

market rinak

married (male) zhenat

(female) zamoozhem

mascara toosh' dlya ryesneets

mass (church) myesa

match (light) speechka

(sports) match

material (cloth) tkan'

mattress matras

maybe mozhet' bit'

me: for me dlya myenya

give it to me dIt-ye mnye

meal yeda

meat myasa

mechanic myekhaneek

medicine lyekarstva

meet fstryechat'

meeting fstryecha

melon dinya

menu myenyoo

message sa-abshyeneeye

midday poldyen'

middle: in the middle pasyeryedeen-ye

midnight polnach'

milk malako

mine: it's mine eta moy

mineral water meenyeral'na-ya vada

minute meenoota

mirror zyerkala

Miss mees

miss (verb: train, etc.) apazdivat'

mistake asheepka

to make a mistake asheebat'sa

mom mama

monastery manastir'

money dyen'gee

month myesyats

monument pamyatneek

moon loona

more bol'she

morning ootra

in the morning ootram

mosaic mazayka

Moscow maskva

mosquito kamar

mother mat'

motorcycle matatseekl

mountain gara

mouse mish'

moustache oosi

mouth rot

move dveegat'sa
  don't move! nye dveegltyes'!
  (house) pyerye-yezhat'

movie feel'm

movie theater keeno

Mr. gaspadeen

Mrs. gaspazha

much mnoga
  not much nyemnoga
  much better/slower garazda
  looch-ye/myedlyenye-ye

mug krooshka

museum moozyay

mushroom greep

music moozika

musical instrument moozikal'ni
  eenstroomyent

musician moozikant

mussels meedee

must dolzhen

mustard garcheetsa

my: my house moy dom
  my bag ma-ya soomka
  my keys ma-ee klyoochee

nail (metal) gvozd'
  (finger) nogat'

nail file peelka dlya nagtyay

nail polish lak dlya nagtyay

name (first) eemya
  (last) fameelee-ya

napkin salfyetka

narrow oozkee

near: near the door okala dvyeree
  near Detroit okala Detroyta

necessary noozhni

neck sheya

necklace azheryel'ye

need (verb) noozhdat'sa
  I need … mnye noozhna …
  there's no need eta nyenoozhna

needle eegla

negative (photo) nyegateef

nephew plyemyaneek

never neekagda

new novi

news novastee

newspaper gazyeta

newsstand gazyetni kee-osk

New Zealand nova-ya zyelandee-ya

New Zealander
  (male) navazyelandyets
  (female) navazyelantka

next slyedooyooshee
  next week na slyedooyooshay
  nyedyel-ye
  next month fslyedooyooshem
  myesyatse
  what next? shto dal'she?

nice preeyatni

niece plyemyaneetsa

night noch'

nightclub nachnoy kloop

nightgown nachna-ya roobashka

night porter nachnoy dyezhoorni

no (response) nyet
  I have no money oo myenya
  nyet dyenyek

noisy shoomni

normal abichni

north syevyer

Northern Ireland syevyerna-ya
  eerlandee-ya

nose nos

not nye

notebook zapeesna-ya kneega

nothing neechyevo
notice ab-yavlyeneeye
novel raman
now tyepyer'
nowhere neegd-ye
number nomyer
nurse myedsyestra
nut *(fruit)* aryekh

occasionally eenagda
occupation prafyesee-ya
occupied zanyat
ocean akye-an
October Revolution aktyebr'ska-ya
   ryevalyootsee-ya
office ofees
often chasta
oil masla
ointment maz'
OK ladna
old stari
olive masleena
omelette amlyet
on na
one adeen
onion look
only tol'ka
open *(verb)* atkrivat'
   (adj.) atkriti
opera opyera
opposite: opposite the hotel
   naproteef gasteeneetsi
optician opteeka
or eelee
orange *(color)* aranzhevi
   (fruit) apyel'seen
orange juice apyel'seenavi sok
orchestra arkyestr
orchestra seats *(theater)* partyer
order *(in restaurant)* zakazivat'
   out of order nye fparyatk-ye
ordinary *(normal)* abichni

other droogoy
our nash
   it's ours eta nashe
out: he's out yevo nyet
outlet shtyepsyel'
outside na ooleets-ye
over nad
   over there tam

pacifier soska
pack of cards kaloda kart
package pakyet
   (parcel) pasilka
packet pachka
page straneetsa
pain bol'
paint *(noun)* kraska
painting karteena
pair para
pajamas peezhama
Pakistani pakeestanskee
palace dvaryets
pale blyedni
pancakes bleeni
pants bryookee
paper boomaga
parents radeetyelee
park *(noun)* park
   (verb) staveet' masheenoo
parking garage garazh
parking lights padfarneekee
part chast'
party *(celebration)* vyechyereenka
   (political) partee-ya
Party member chlyen partee
pass *(traffic)* abganyat'
passenger pasazheer
passport pasport
path trapeenka
pavement tratoo-ar
pay plateet'
peace meer

peach pyerseek

peanuts arakhees

pear groosha

pearl zhemchook

peas garokh

pedestrian pyeshekhot

pen roochka

pencil karandash

penknife pyeracheeni nosh

pensioner pyensee-anyer

people lyoodee

people's narodni

pepper pyeryets

per: per night zanach'

perestroika pyeryestroyka

perfect pryevaskhodni

perfume dookhee

perhaps mozhet bit'

perm zaveefka pyermanyent

permission razryesheneeye

pharmacy aptyeka

photograph
  (noun) fatagrafee-ya
  (verb) fatagrafeeravat'

photographer fatograf

phrase book razgavorneek

piano fartyep'yana

picnic peekneek

piece koosok

pillow padooshka

pilot peelot

pin boolafka

pine (tree) sasna

pineapple ananas

ping-pong peeng-pong

pink rozavi

pipe (for smoking) troopka
  (for water) troobaprovat

pizza peetsa

place myesta

plain prastoy

plant rastyeneeye

plastic plasteekavi

plastic bag plasteekavi pakyet

plate taryelka

platform platforma

play (noun: theater) p'yesa
  (verb) eegrat'

please pazhalsta

plug (sink) propka

plum sleeva

pocket karman

poison atravlyeneeye

Poland pol'sha

police meeleetsee-ya

policeman meeleetsee-anyer

police station atdyelyeneeye
  meeleetsee-ya

politics paleeteeka

pollution zagryaznyeneeye

poor byedni
  (bad quality) plakhoy

pop music pop moozika

popular papoolyarni

pork sveeneena

port (harbor) port

porter (for baggage) naseel'sheek

possible vazmozhni

postcard atkritka

poster plakat

post office pochta

potato kartofyel'

potato chips khroostyashee kartofyel'

poultry pteetsa

pound foont

powder (washing) parashok
  (talcum) poodra

prawn kryevyetka

pregnant byeryemyena-ya

prescription ryetsyept

present padarak

pretty kraseevi

price tsyena

priest svyashyeneek

private chasni

problem prablyema

profession prafyesee-ya

public abshyestveni

pull tyanoot'

puncture prakol

pure cheesti

purple fee-alyetavi

purse kashelyok

push tolkat'

put klast'

quality kachyestva

quantity kaleechyestva

question vapros

quick bistri

quiet teekhee

quite *(fairly)* davol'na

  (fully) safsyem

radiator bataryeya

radio radee-o

radish ryedeeska

railroad line
zhelyezna-darozhna-ya leenee-ya

rain dosht'

raincoat plash'

raisins eezyoom

rare *(uncommon)* ryetkee

  (steak) skrov'yoo

rat krisa

razor breetva

razor blades breetvyeniye lyezvee-ya

read cheetat'

ready gatof

real nastayashee

receipt chyek

receive paloochat'

receptionist dyezhoorni

recommend ryekamyendavat'

record *(music)* plasteenka

  (sports, etc.) ryekort

record player pra-eegrivatyel'

red krasni

Red Army krasna-ya armee-ya

Red Square krasna-ya ploshat'

refrigerator khaladeel'neek

relative rodstvyeneek

relax atdikhat'

religion ryeleegee-ya

remember pomneet'

  I don't remember ya nye pomnyoo

rent *(verb)* naneemat'

reservation zakas

reservation office kasa

reserve zakazivat'

rest *(remainder)* astatak

  (relax) otdikh

restaurant ryestaran

restroom too-alyet

  (men's) moozhskoy too-alyet

  (women's) zhenskee too-alyet

return *(come back)* vazvrashat'sa

  (give back) vazvrashat'

rice rees

rich bagati

right *(correct)* praveel'ni

  (direction) pravi

  on the right naprava

ring *(wedding, etc.)* kal'tso

ripe zryeli

river ryeka

road daroga

rock *(stone)* skala

  (music) rok

roll *(bread)* boolachka

Romania roominee-ya

roof krisha

room komnata

  (in hotel) nomyer

  (space) myesta

rope vyeryofka

rose roza

round *(circular)* kroogli

  it's my round moy chyeryot

round-trip ticket abratni beelyet

rowboat vyosyel'na-ya lotka
rubber (*material*) ryezeena
ruby (*stone*) roobeen
rug (*mat*) kovreek
  (*blanket*) adyeyala
ruins roo-eeni
ruler (*for drawing*) leenyayka
rum rom
run (*person*) byezhat'
Russia rasee-ya
Russian (*adj.*) rooskee
  (*man*) rooskee
  (*woman*) rooska-ya
Russian Orthodox Church
  rooska-ya pravaslavna-ya tserkaf'

sad groosni
safe byezapasni
safety pin angleeska-ya boolafka
salad salat
salami kapchyona-ya kalbasa
sale (*at reduced prices*)
  raspradazha
salesperson pradavyets
salmon lasos'
salt sol'
same: the same dress to zhe plat'ye
  the same people tye zhe lyoodee
samovar samavar
sand pyesok
sandals sandalee
sandwich bootyerbrot
sanitary napkins
  geegee-yeneechyeskeeye salfyetkee
sauce so-oos
saucepan kastryoolya
saucer blyoots-ye
sauna sa-oona
sausage saseeska
say gavareet'
  what did you say? shto vi skazalee?
  how do you say ...? kak boodyet ...?

scarf sharf
  (*head*) platok
scent dookhee
school shkola
scissors nozhneetsi
score shyot
Scotland shatlandee-ya
Scotsman shatlandyets
Scotswoman shatlantka
Scottish shatlantskee
screw veent
screwdriver atvyortka
sculpture skool'ptoora
sea mor-ye
seafood marskeeye pradookti
seat myesta
second syekoonda
  (*in series*) ftaroy
second floor ftaroy etash
see veedyet'
  I can't see ya nye veezhoo
  I see! nomnyoo!
seem kazat'sa
sell pradavat'
send pasilat'
separate atdyel'ni
serious syer'yozni
serve absloozheevat'
service (*restaurant*) absloozheevaneeye
  (*church*) sloozhba
several nyeskal'ka
sew sheet'
shade tyen'
shallow myelkee
shampoo shampoon'
shape forma
sharp ostri
shave (*noun*) breet'yo
  (*verb*) breet'sa
shaving cream kryem dlya breet'ya
shawl shal'
she ana
sheet prastinya

sherry khyeryes
ship parakhot
shirt roobashka
shoelaces shnoorkee
shoe polish kryem dlya oboovee
shoes tooflee
shop magazeen
shore byerek
short karotkee
shorts shorti
shoulder plyecho
show pakazivat'
shower (bath) doosh
shrimp kryevyetka
shut (verb) zakrivat'
Siberia seebeer'
sick (ill) bal'noy
  I feel sick ya plokha syebya
  choostvoo-yoo
side (edge) starana
sights: the sights of …
  dasta-preemyechatyel'nastee …
sign znak
silk shyolk
silver (metal) syeryebro
simple prastoy
sing pyet'
single (one) adeen
  (unmarried: male) khalastoy
  (female) nyezamoozhnya-ya
single room adnamyesni nomyer
sink rakaveena
sister syestra
sit down sadeet'sa
size razmyer
ski (verb) katat'sa na lizhakh
skid (verb) zanaseet'
skirt yoopka
skis lizhee
sky nyeba
sleep (noun) son
  (verb) spat'
  to go to bed lazheet'sa spat'

sleeper spal'ni vagon
sleeping bag spal'ni myeshok
sleeping pill snatvorna-ye
slippers tapachkee
slow myedlyeni
small malyen'kee
smell (noun) zapakh
  (verb) pakhnoot'
smile (noun) oolipka
  (verb) oolibat'sa
smoke (noun) dim
  (verb) kooreet'
snack zakooska
snow snyek
  it's snowing eedyot snyek
snowplow snyega-ooborachna-ya
  masheena
snowstorm snyezhna-ya boorya
so: so good tak kharasho
soap milo
soccer footbol
soccer ball footbol'ni myach
socialism satsee-aleezm
socks naskee
soda water gazeerovana-ya vada
somebody kto-ta
somehow kak-ta
something shto-ta
sometimes eenagda
somewhere gdye-ta
son sin
song pyesnya
sorry! eezveeneet-ye!
  I'm sorry eezveeneet-ye
soup soop
south yook
souvenir soovyeneer
Soviet savyetskee
Soviet Union savyetskee sayoos
spade (shovel) lapata
spark plug zapal'na-ya svyecha

speak gavar<u>ee</u>t'
  do you speak …?
  vi gavar<u>ee</u>t-ye pa-…?
  I don't speak … ya nye
  gavar<u>yoo</u> pa-…
spend (*money*) trat<u>ee</u>t'
  (*time*) pravad<u>ee</u>t'
spider pa-<u>oo</u>k
spinach shpeenat
spine speen<u>a</u>
spoon l<u>o</u>shka
sport sp<u>o</u>rt
sprain rastyazh<u>e</u>neeye
spring (*mechanical*) ryes<u>o</u>ra
spy shpee-<u>o</u>n
square (*town*) pl<u>o</u>shat'
stadium stadee-<u>o</u>n
stage sts<u>ye</u>na
stairs l<u>ye</u>sneetsa
stamp m<u>a</u>rka
stand (*verb*) st<u>a</u>yat'
star zvyezd<u>a</u>
  (*film*) keenazvyezd<u>a</u>
start (*verb*) nach<u>ee</u>nat'
station (*main-line terminal*) vagz<u>a</u>l
  (*subway*) st<u>a</u>ntsee-ya
statue stat<u>oo</u>-ya
stay (*verb*) astan<u>a</u>vleevat'sa
steak beefsht<u>ye</u>ks
steal krast'
  it's been stolen ookr<u>a</u>lee
Steppes st<u>ye</u>p'
sting (*noun*) ook<u>oo</u>s
  (*verb*) koos<u>a</u>t'
  it stings zhy<u>o</u>t'
stockings choolk<u>ee</u>
stomach zhel<u>oo</u>dak
stomachache bol' vzhel<u>oo</u>tk-ye
stop (*something*) astan<u>a</u>vleevat'
  (*come to a halt*) astan<u>a</u>vleevat'sa
  bus stop astan<u>o</u>fka
  stop! st<u>o</u>y!
storm b<u>oo</u>rya

strawberry kloobn<u>ee</u>ka
stream (*small river*) roochy<u>ay</u>
street <u>oo</u>leetsa
string (*cord*) vyery<u>o</u>fka
  (*guitar, etc.*) stroon<u>a</u>
student (*male*) stood<u>ye</u>nt
  (*female*) stood<u>ye</u>ntka
stupid gl<u>oo</u>pi
suburbs pr<u>ee</u>garat
subway myetr<u>o</u>
suddenly vdrook
sugar s<u>a</u>khar
suit (*noun*) kast<u>yoo</u>m
  (*verb*) eet<u>ee</u>
  it suits you vam eed<u>yo</u>t
suitcase chyemad<u>a</u>n
sun s<u>o</u>ntse
sunbathe zagar<u>a</u>t'
sunburn s<u>o</u>lnyechni azh<u>o</u>k
sunglasses s<u>o</u>lnyechniye achk<u>ee</u>
sunny: it's sunny s<u>o</u>lnyechna
suntan zag<u>a</u>r
suntan lotion m<u>a</u>sla dlya zag<u>a</u>ra
supermarket ooneevyers<u>a</u>m
supper <u>oo</u>zheen
supplement dapaln<u>ye</u>neeye
sure oov<u>ye</u>reni
  are you sure? vi oov<u>ye</u>reni?
surname fam<u>ee</u>lee-ya
surprise (*verb*) oodeevl<u>ya</u>t'
sweat (*noun*) pot
  (*verb*) pat<u>ye</u>t'
sweater dzh<u>e</u>mpyer
sweet (*not sour*) sl<u>a</u>tkee
swim pl<u>a</u>vat'
swimming pool bas<u>ya</u>yn
swimming trunks pl<u>a</u>fkee
switch viklyooch<u>a</u>tyel'
synagogue seen<u>a</u>goga

table stol
tablet tabl<u>ye</u>tka
taillights z<u>a</u>dneeye f<u>a</u>ri

take brat'

take off (*noun*) atpravlyeneeye

talcum powder tal'k

talk (*noun*) razgavor

  (*verb*) razgavareevat'

tall visokee

tampon tampon

tap kran

tape (*adhesive, invisible*) klyayka-ya lyenta

taste fkoos

tea chI

team kamanda

telegram tyelyegrama

telephone (*noun*) tyelyefon

  (*verb*) zvaneet'

telephone booth tyelyefon-aftamat

telephone call tyelyefoni zvanok

television tyelyeveezar

temperature tyempyeratoora

tennis tyenees

tent palatkathan chyem

thank (*verb*) blagadareet'

  thanks, thank you spaseeba

that: that bus tot aftoboos

  that woman ta zhensheena

  what's that? shto eta?

  I think that ... ya dooma-yoo shto ...

theater tyeatr

their: their room eekh komnata

  it's theirs eta eekh

them: for them dlya neekh

  give it to them atdIt-ye eem

then tagda

there tam

  there is/are ... eemye-yetsa/eemye-yootsa ...

  is/are there ...? zdyes' est' ...?

  is there a bank here? zdyes' yest' bank?

thermometer gradoosneek

these: these things etee vyeshee

  these are mine eta ma-ee

they anee

  it's they eta anee

thick (*wide*) tolsti

thief vor

thin tonkee

thing vyesh'

think doomat'

  I think so ya dooma-yoo shto da

  I'll think about it ya padooma-yoo ab etam

third trye'tee

thirsty: I'm thirsty ya khachoo peet'

this: this bus etat aftoboos

  this woman eta zhensheena

  what's this? shto eta?

  this is Mr. ... eta gaspadeen ...

those: those things tye vyeshee

  those are his eta yevo

throat gorla

through chyeryes

thumbtack knopka

thunderstorm graza

ticket beelyet

ticket office beelyetna-ya kasa

tie (*noun*) galstook

  (*verb*) zavyazivat'

tights kalgotkee

time vryemya

  what's the time? katori chas?

timetable raspeesaneeye

tip (*money*) cha-yeviye

tired oostali

  I'm tired (*male*) ya oostal

  (*female*) ya oostala

tissues boomazhniye salfyetkee

to: to America vamereekoo

  to the station na vagzal

  to the doctor k vrachoo

toast padzharyeni khlyep

tobacco tabak

today syevodnya

together fmyest-ye

toilet too-alyet

toilet paper too-alyetna-ya boomaga
tomato pameedor
tomato juice tamatni sok
tomorrow zaftra
tongue yazik
tonic toneek
tonight syevodnya vyechyeram
too (also) tagzhe
  (excessive) sleeshkam
tooth zoop
toothache zoobna-ya bol'
toothbrush zoobna-ya shyotka
toothpaste zoobna-ya pasta
touch trogat'
tour ekskoorsee-ya
tourist tooreest
tourist office tooreesteechyeska-ye byooro
towel palatyentse
tower bashnya
town gorat
town hall ratoosha
toy eegrooshka
tractor traktar
tradition tradeetsee-ya
traffic ooleechna-ye dveezheneeye
traffic jam propka
train po-yest
tram tramvI
Trans-Siberian Express trans-seebeerskee ekspres
translate pyeryevadeet'
travel pootyeshestvavat'
travel agency byooro pootyeshestvee
traveler's check darozhni chyek
tray padnos
tree dyeryeva
trolley tralyayboos
truck groozaveek
trunk (car) bagashneek
truth pravda

try (experimentally) probavat'
  (endeavor) starat'sa
tunnel toonyel'
Turkmenistan toorkmyenee-ya
turn pavaracheevat'
turn signal ookazatyel' pavarota
tweezers peentset
typewriter peeshoosha-ya masheenka

Ukraine ookra-eena
umbrella zonteek
uncle dyadya
uncomfortable nye-oodobni
under pod
underpants troosi
understand paneemat'
  I don't understand ya nye paneema-yoo
underwear neezhnye-ye byel'yo
United States sa-yedeenyoniye shtati
university ooneevyerseetyet
unmarried (male) nyezhenat
  (female) nyezamoozhem
until do
unusual nye-abichni
upward navyerkh
upstairs navyerkhoo
Urals ooral
urgent srochni
us: it's for us eta dlya nas
  give it to us dIt-ye nam
use (noun) oopatryeblyeneeye
  (verb) oopatryeblyat'
  it's no use nye rabota-yet
useful palyezni
useless byespalyezni
USSR es-es-es-er
usual abichni
usually abichna

vacant (room) svabodni
vacuum cleaner pilyesos

valid dyaystv<u>ee</u>tyel'ni
valley dal<u>ee</u>na
valve kl<u>a</u>pan
vanilla van<u>ee</u>l'
vase v<u>a</u>za
veal tyely<u>a</u>teena
vegetable <u>o</u>vash
vegetarian *(person)* vyegyetaree<u>a</u>nyets
very <u>o</u>chyen'
vest m<u>i</u>ka
view veet
villa v<u>ee</u>la
village dyer<u>ye</u>vnya
vinegar <u>oo</u>ksoos
violin skr<u>ee</u>pka
visa v<u>ee</u>za
visit *(noun)* pasyeshy<u>e</u>neeye
  (verb) pasyesh<u>a</u>t'
visitor pasyet<u>ee</u>tyel'
  (tourist) toor<u>ee</u>st
vitamin veetam<u>ee</u>n
vodka v<u>o</u>tka
voice g<u>o</u>las
voltage napryazh<u>e</u>neeye

wait zhdat'
waiter afeetsee-<u>a</u>nt
  waiter! afeetsee-<u>a</u>nt!
waiting room zal azheed<u>a</u>nee-ya
waitress afeetsee-<u>a</u>ntka
Wales oo<u>e</u>l's
walk
  (noun: stroll) prag<u>oo</u>lka
  (verb) gool<u>ya</u>t'
  to go for a walk eet<u>ee</u> na
  prag<u>oo</u>lkoo
wall sty<u>e</u>na
wallet boom<u>a</u>shneek
want khat<u>ye</u>t'
  I want … ya khach<u>oo</u> …
war vln<u>a</u>
wardrobe shkaf
warm t<u>yo</u>pli

was: I was *(male)* ya bil
  (female) ya bil<u>a</u>
  it was <u>e</u>ta b<u>i</u>la
wasp as<u>a</u>
watch *(noun)* chas<u>i</u>
  (verb) smatr<u>ye</u>t'
water vad<u>a</u>
  drinking water peet'yeva-ya vad<u>a</u>
waterfall vadap<u>a</u>d
wave *(noun)* valn<u>a</u>
  (verb) makh<u>a</u>t'
we mi
weather pag<u>o</u>da
wedding sv<u>a</u>d'ba
week nyed<u>ye</u>lya
welcome dabr<u>o</u> pazhal<u>a</u>vat'
  you're welcome pazh<u>a</u>lsta
Welsh oo<u>e</u>l'skee
were: we were mi b<u>i</u>lee
  you were *(plural, formal)* vi b<u>i</u>lee
  (singular, familiar) (male) ti bil
  (female) ti bil<u>a</u>
  they were an<u>ee</u> b<u>i</u>lee
west z<u>a</u>pat
  in the West na z<u>a</u>pad-ye
wet m<u>o</u>kri
what? shto?
wheel kaly<u>e</u>s<u>o</u>
wheelchair eenval<u>ee</u>edna-ya kal<u>ya</u>ska
when? k<u>a</u>gda?
where? gdye?
which? kak<u>o</u>y?
while pak<u>a</u>
whiskey v<u>ee</u>skee
white b<u>ye</u>li
who? kto?
whole ts<u>e</u>li
whose? chyay?
why? pachyem<u>oo</u>?
wide sheer<u>o</u>kee
wife zhen<u>a</u>
wild d<u>ee</u>kee
win vi<u>ee</u>grivat'
wind v<u>ye</u>tyer

125

window akno

wine veeno

wing krilo

wish zhelat'

with s

without byez

woman zhensheena

wonderful choodyesni

wood dyeryeva

wool shyerst'

word slova

work (noun) rabota
   (verb) rabotat'

worry (verb) val'navat'sa

worse khoozhe

worst khoodshee

wrapping paper abyortachna-ya
   boomaga

wrench gayechni klyooch

wrist zapyast'ye

writing paper pachtova-ya boomaga

wrong nyepraveel'ni

year got

yellow zholti

yes da

yesterday fchyera

yet yeshyo
   not yet yeshyo nyet

you vi
   (singular, familiar) ti

your vash
   (singular, familiar) tvoy
   your book vasha/tvaya kneega
   your shoes vashee/tva-ee tooflee

yours: is this yours? eta vashe?/tvayo?

Yugoslavian yoogaslafskee

zip molnee-ya

zoo zapark